MW00606093

Tribute

"If Mercedes had embraced you, you'd never forget it. She had the ability to embrace people like no one else in the world; one always had the feeling of being embraced by Mother Earth herself. She took all of us in her arms with her voice, with this unequaled bel canto voice, which was always a pure expression of her soul. There was never anything artificial about this wonderful woman, this brave woman, this icon of courageous resistance to military dictatorship. For me, she radiated the most important thing that makes a great human being: kindness." - **Konstantin Wecker, singer and poet, Germany**

Endorsements

"In this work, you will find a new and touching perspective on our beloved Mercedes. It is a heartfelt and affectionate tribute honoring the life of my mother. Thank you, Anette, for all your efforts in the name of the Mercedes Sosa Foundation."
-Fabián Matus, son of Mercedes Sosa and president of The Mercedes Sosa Foundation.

"The Author's profound connection with Mercedes Sosa and subsequent transformation is a testament of the restoring impact of positive connections. The author does more than just entertain the reader or spark the reader's interest. She spreads hope and knowledge."
-Pauline Skeates, Therapist, Director of Insight-International and Developer of Insight Focused Therapy, New Zealand

Mercedes Sosa
The Voice of Hope

Anette Christensen

Mercedes Sosa
The Voice of Hope

My life-transforming encounter

Tribute2Life
PUBLISHING

No part of this book may be reproduced in any written, electronic, recording, or photocopying without written permission of the publisher or author. The exception would be in the case of brief quotations embodied in the critical articles or reviews and pages where permission is specifically granted by the publisher or author. Although every precaution has been taken to verify the accuracy of the information contained herein, the author and publisher assume no responsibility for any errors or omissions. No liability is assumed for damages that may result from the use of information contained within.

Publisher: Tribute2Life Publishing
Editors: NY Book Editors & David Larkin
Cover Design: © Tribute2Life Design
Cover Photo: © Bernd Arnold
Back Page Cover Photo: © Reuters/Oswaldo Riwas
Interior Design: © Tribute2Life Design
Chapter Opening Illustrations: © Monica Gaifem
Inside Photos: © Reuter Archives & The Mercedes Sosa Foundation
Inside Drawings: © Anette Christensen
Author Photograph: © Pernille Schmidt
Set with: Lora Font & Antonio Font
ISBN:
978-87-998216-5-5 (Paperback)
978-87-998216-4-8 (eBook)
First Editions

Mercedes Sosa-The Voice of Hope by Anette Christensen
© 2019 by Anette Christensen. All rights reserved.

Dedication

For my husband, Kåre. I see who you are, and you will always be beautiful in my eyes. You make me feel I'm the most loved woman in the world, and your love makes me shine. My soul has found its home with you.

Acknowledgements

Thanks to Serhan, "My Turkish Miracle." You believed in me, motivated me, inspired me, and fueled me with energy to complete this book. Your friendship and trust are priceless.

Thanks to my supportive family and caring friends who have blown wind in my sails in so many different ways over the years. I can't mention you all, but you know who you are!

Thanks to Sandy Fabrin from Insight Focused Therapy for assisting me with insight on the psychological aspects of the book.

Thanks to my investors for believing in my project and making it possible for me to work and engage with world class editors.

Thanks to David Larkin for engaging wholeheartedly in the final editing of the book, for understanding where I wanted to go, and for gently guiding me toward my goal.

Contents

Introduction

I T IS AMAZING how much power people have to influence our lives, for better or for worse, and how, sometimes, it can happen out of the blue in the most unexpected of ways. Mercedes Sosa, the world-class Argentine singer and activist, had that effect on me—and strangely enough, it was on the day she died.

I first heard of Mercedes Sosa when her death was announced on the news. I was at my lowest in almost every way you can imagine. The financial crisis had forced my husband and me to close our two companies, a travel agency and a real estate agency. We were compelled to sell our house, and, around the same time, I was diagnosed with Chronic Fatigue Syndrome, leaving me unable to work and pay off our debts. As a result, I was feeling psychologically distressed and didn't have any hope left for a better future. I also struggled to recover from childhood traumas that had left my mother and I estranged for a while.

It was in the depth of my uttermost desperation that my discovery of Mercedes Sosa sparked a new hope that launched my recovery. As her death was announced on the news, I watched a short performance of her singing "Gracias a la vida" (Thanks to Life). It was a defining moment. The intensity and firmness in her voice, the intoning of every note and every word reached me like glassy water reflecting my soul. Her tenderness, profound passion, immense presence, and charisma moved me deeply, and this short sequence took me on a journey that changed my life.

I started to watch and listen to Mercedes Sosa on the internet and soon I found myself completely immersed in her life,- a universe of music and love. In the beginning, I did it solely for my own comfort and recovery. The idea of writing a book about her and how my encounter with her affected my life only occurred to me three years later, when I knew that I had discovered a road to personal wholeness that really worked—and that there was scientific evidence backing my experience.

The Chronic Fatigue I suffered from had forced me to slow down in every way. This was very frustrating until I realized that slowing down enabled me to be more aware of my inner voice, which led me to relate to Mercedes Sosa as a mother figure. Intuitively, I began to use her eyes like a mirror that reflected back to me what I had missed out on as a child. In her eyes I saw the glance of a mother, a glance that said, "I see who you are, and in my eyes you are wonderful."

My recovery took place as I practiced mindfulness. Our thoughts are like bales strewn all over the place in a dark warehouse, and practicing mindfulness is like turning on the lights so we can navigate without bumping into them and getting hurt. Most of our thoughts happen automatically and have enormous power to influence our mood, feelings, and behavior. To be mindful means to step back and observe our thoughts and feelings without judging them or believing they are facts.

When I practiced mindfulness, painful memories from my childhood sometimes emerged. As I focused my attention on Mercedes Sosa, my whole being became peaceful and relaxed. Naturally, I became curious to find out why Mercedes and her music had this effect on me.

Drawing on research into interpersonal neurobiology, I reveal my findings about how connecting with another person can result in personal transformation and growth and how it can happen even in an imaginary relation, as I had to Mercedes Sosa. Neuroscience stresses that what we focus on will shape our brain, which in turn changes our experience of the world and how we perceive our past. My personal story in part two shows how I used my envisioned relationship with Mercedes Sosa to change the neural firing in my brain and rewrite my past. It spells out the avenue of healing I found, a path that can easily be accessed by anyone. It would be my greatest joy if my experience touches you and can be useful to you too.

I feel that if I don't share my story with you now, I will be doing a disservice, not only to Mercedes Sosa, but to her voice of hope that lives on in each of us. I also feel I owe it to anyone who struggles with emotional traumas or chronic pain because what I have encountered can work for everyone—whether it happens by connecting with Mercedes or another significant person. I invite you into my personal journey to explore why my connection with Mercedes became crucial, and I'll let you in on the secrets that I didn't share with anyone for years.

Since my discovery of Mercedes Sosa had such a deep and haunting impact on me, I began searching for any bit of information I could find about her. I soon learned that I wasn't alone with the experience of being invigorated and transformed in her presence. She was the voice of hope not only to me but to millions of fans as well. As I delved deep into Mercedes' life I discovered that her fans often referred to her as a "mystical presence." This aroused my curiosity to gain a better understanding of her personal life—her relationships with her family, fans, and friends as well as the events that shaped her life on a personal and professional level. I embarked on a quest to find the secret behind her enormous impact and this so-called "mystical presence." What I discovered affected me on various levels. Watching how Mercedes dealt with social and political problems increased my social awareness. Witnessing how she related to others, whether it was peasants or presidents, friends or foes, touched me deeply and aroused a desire in me to become more respectful and compassionate and to pay full attention to others. But most importantly, her example inspired me to get in touch with my inner self, nurture my wounds, embrace the past, and accept the unexpected changes that life brings. If Mercedes could bounce back from her afflictions as a more empathic, resilient, and authentic person, so can each of us once we learn to respond to life's challenges in a constructive way.

While writing this book, I reached out to Sosa's family in Argentina in hopes of receiving some insights into her life as well as to receive their blessing on this project of documenting her life, upbringing, career in music, and the social and political environment she lived in. I am very happy that they approved of the book at a very early stage and found my psychological approach enticing.

I also engaged with some of Mercedes Sosa's personal friends and fans and have included their stories as well. Through my connection with the Latin American people I began to understand Mercedes Sosa's deep affection towards her people. The Latin American people have become very special to me too and their love, support and encouragement has touched my heart.

I do not consider this book to be a complete biography of Mercedes Sosa—rather it is a personal profile of her. I have used my imagination in a few places to fill in some of the gaps without reducing the credibility of the overall story. These passages are listed in the addendum. Here I also explain how I used a mindful approach to get to know Mercedes well enough to write this book without having access to the Spanish sources.

Maybe you wonder why I'm making the effort to describe the political situation in South America. Through Mercedes, I developed an affection for South America and realized that the continent is much overlooked in the media outside the Spanish-speaking world. As Mercedes Sosa's friend, the Cuban singer Pablo Milanés once said, it is not possible to tell the story of Latin America without mentioning Mercedes Sosa. I believe the opposite is true as well. It is not possible to tell about Mercedes Sosa without telling about this troubled but vibrant continent in which Mercedes invested her entire life. I refer to South America as the continent in the western hemisphere consisting of the countries and islands south of Panama. I use Latin America as a cultural entity of Spanish and Portuguese speaking nations in both Americas.

The drawings throughout the book are my own. I am not an artist, and I have never taken a single drawing lesson. But as I watched and listened to Mercedes Sosa, I started to put down on paper my vision of her. It became a form of therapy to me.

On my YouTube Channel, Mercedes Sosa – The Voice of Hope, you will find a playlist with many of the songs and episodes that I describe in the book. As you come across these songs, I encourage you to visit the channel so that you may fully appreciate what is being described.

I am excited that after almost nine years of recovering, pondering, listening, watching, researching, and writing, I can finally introduce you to this amazing woman who influenced an entire continent by using her unique talent and outstanding personality and who turned my life around even after her death.

I have written this book out of deep respect for Mercedes Sosa and everything she stands for. This is my love song to Mercedes Sosa. In her voice, life becomes a song with a scent of hope as sweet and beautiful as the flower that grows in the paths of those who looks forward. Her voice represents a woman who in turn represents dreams, ideals and love that go far beyond the border of music. Mercedes Sosa was more than song. She was the voice of hope to many. May this book extend her voice and the hope she kindled.

Part One

Mercedes Sosa's
Life and Career

"The most beautiful people we have known are those who have known defeat, known suffering, known struggle, known loss, and have found their way out of the depths. These persons have an appreciation, sensitivity and an understanding of life that fills them with compassion, gentleness, and a deep loving concern. Beautiful people do not just happen."
Elisabeth Kübler-Ross

Denmark,
October 4, 2009

"The Argentine singer and folk heroine Mercedes Sosa has died from multiple organ failure at a hospital in Buenos Aires after being admitted three weeks ago. Her career spanned over six decades and she recorded more than forty albums, performing all over the world. Sosa was the underground reference point for many Argentines during the time of dictatorship, and through her songs she gave life to the protest movement among the working class, a movement which led to the collapse of the military junta in 1983. Mercedes Sosa became famous in Europe when she was living in exile in Spain and France from 1979 to 1982. She lived to seventy-four years old."

I T'S A SUNDAY evening and I settle to watch the news with my husband. Along with a report of Mercedes Sosa's death, a short film clip of a beautiful lady with long, dark hair, wearing a black dress with a red Andean poncho on top comes up on the TV screen. With extraordinary passion and a voice remarkable and soulful, she sings a song, "Gracias a la vida" (Thanks to Life). I become captivated by her authenticity and charisma, and it takes only but a short while to realize I am watching a genuine and sincere woman so pure and extraordinary that I begin to wonder why I haven't heard of her before now. As if nothing else matters, I get up to use the internet and find out more about this lady. An enormous number of YouTube links come up. I begin to watch and listen.

In the first clip, Mercedes sings "Zamba por vos" (Zamba for You) ever so gloriously with the Argentine folklore quartet, Los Chalchaleros. Radiant and graceful as a gentle embrace Mercedes arrives onstage with a consolatory smile on her lips and a sparkle of vitality in her eyes. To unending applause she proceeds to greet the members of the group, drawing them into warm embraces. Then she turns to the crowd and with a calm demeanor, starts singing in her contralto voice–deep, pleasant, and soft.

The second clip I watch is "Todo cambia" (Everything Changes), recorded at the Festival de Viña in Chile, 1993. Dressed in black from top to toe, she appears mystical and monumental, sounding just as powerful and convincing as she looks. I sense a tremendous energy emanating from her as she conquers the stage with her Latin American dancing steps and her scarf swinging above her head. I see a dynamic and forthright person who is unafraid of expressing her true self. The sincere and tender yet firm look in her eyes captivates me, and I feel as though she is looking directly into my soul through the computer screen. There is something about her, a "mystical presence," which reaches to the deepest parts of my being, and my well of longing. Tears stream down my face as I realize I have encountered something that I have always hoped to find.

I instinctively know that she is a singer with a message and a mission. I want to find out what they are.

Buenos Aires,
October 4, 2009

FOLLOWING THE President's official announcement marking the start of three national days of mourning, the flags are flown at half-mast all over Argentina. Across the country concerts and shows scheduled during this period are cancelled, and condolences from heads of state—in Latin America and the rest of the world—pour in.

"La Negra" (The Black One), as she was fondly called owing to her jet black hair and her Northern Argentine, Andean ancestry, lies peacefully in her casket in the most formal room of the Congress, the "Salón de los Pasos Perdidos," an honor reserved for only the most prominent of national icons. On *Avenida Callao*, the street leading to the Congress, admirers line up to pay their respects.[1]

In the Pasos Perdidos, lavish wreaths adorn the impressive marble hall. Gigantic chandeliers and massive candles light up the dimness of the high-ceilinged room with the uncovered casket positioned right in the center. Argentina's president, Cristina Fernández de Kirchner, accompanies Sosa's family as they pay homage to the singer. The family, including Mercedes' son, Fabián Matus, and her two grandchildren, Agustín and Araceli, stand closely with their arms around each other as though in a half-embrace while Cristina caresses Mercedes Sosa's lifeless hand. Christina's husband, the former President Néstor Kirchner, stands rather guardedly by her side with a cautious look.

Ordinary people are there too. Respectfully, a growing flock of mourners pass by the open casket where she is seen resting in her embroidered blue dress. Her long, black hair, which at the age of seventy-four, doesn't have a single strand of gray in it, frames her calm, high-cheekbone face. Her hands are carefully folded on her stomach around a bouquet of white roses. Singer Argentino Luna plays her songs as weeping fans sing along and take turns to leave flowers by her coffin.

October 5, 2009

FABIÁN AND Mercedes' closest relatives follow the brown wooden casket as it is carried out to the hearse parked outside the Congress. All along Avenida Rivadavia, crowds of mourners, of all ages, gather to watch the hearse take her on her last journey, from the Congress to the crematorium. They stand united in a moment of Argentine history that dissolves social and political boundaries.

The procession of hearses drives past slowly and a number of mourners carry banners that say adorable things about her. An old revolutionary in his sixties is holding up a banner that reads, "Thank you for your life and your struggle." A number of people can be seen clapping and waving the Argentine flag with graceful enthusiasm. The young make happy noises, chanting, "*Olé Olé Olé Olé, Negra Negra*," in repeated fashion as though it were the national soccer team returning after winning a championship. At virtually every corner, groups of people bearing different instruments start to sing. Beautiful music echoes through the streets of Buenos Aires—music that has provided hope and comfort for decades, challenging tyranny and fostering democracy.

It is a day of sorrow that reaches deep into the Argentine soul. The national folk heroine, the mother of the nation, is dead. But what she gave through her life and her songs will never die. They live on.

The procession slowly leaves the Congress. The first hearses carry all the flower decorations. The last carries the casket.

Top left: The body of Mercedes Sosa lies in a coffin at a wake in the Congress building in Buenos Aires, October 4, 2009.

Bottom left: People line up outside the Congress to pay their respects to Mercedes Sosa, in Buenos Aires, October 4, 2009.

Top right: Fabian Matus, son of Mercedes Sosa, and friends carry the coffin of Mercedes Sosa during her funeral in Buenos Aires, October 5, 2009.

Top left: People line the street to bid farewell as the hearse carrying the coffin of Mercedes Sosa moves from the Congress building to the cemetery in Buenos Aires, October 5, 2009.

Bottom left: People chant and sing as they line the street to bid farewell as the hearse carrying the coffin of Mercedes Sosa moves from the Congress building to the cemetery.

Top right: A man holds up a banner that reads "Thanks Negra for your songs and your fight" as he waits outside the Congress to pay his respects to Mercedes Sosa.

A *woman holds a picture of Mercedes Sosa at Chacarita cemetery in Buenos Aires, October 5, 2009.*

Time before Exile

San Miguel, Tucumán, July 9, 1935

AT SANTILLÁN HOSPITAL, in northwest Argentina, twenty-four-year-old Ema del Carmen Girón has just given birth. It is seven o'clock in the morning. Her newborn daughter is safely asleep in her arms. The baby announced her entrance into the world with a hefty squall that could be heard all over the maternity ward. What no one knows is that one of history's best voices has just made its first sound. Ema is grateful for this new and precious life she is holding in her arms, and, for a while, she forgets all the financial challenges that will come with raising a child. Ema has a job as a laundress, and her husband, Ernesto Quiterio Sosa, works in the sugar industry harvesting sugarcane and shoveling coal into the oven at the Tucumán Mill.

Through the half-open window, Ema can hear cannon salutes in the distance. She counts them—twenty-one. July 9 is Argentine Independence Day. Ema's instinct is that it is not a coincidence that her daughter is born on this day. She confides in the midwife, who has just come back to the room, "This girl is going to be someone with great influence one day. Her birth is being welcomed by twenty-one salutes."[2] She keeps this conviction in her heart from this moment on.

Ema AND her husband, Ernesto, usually agree on every-thing, but when they have to give their newborn daughter a name, they run into some trouble. Ema wants to call her Marta, while Ernesto opts for Mercedes, after his mother, and Haydeé, after a well-liked cousin. Ultimately she gets the name Haydeé Mercedes Sosa, but for the rest of her life her mother will stubbornly call her Marta.[3]

Mercedes grows up in Tucumán, which is also called the Garden of the Republic. A semi-tropical and agricultural re-gion with countless fields of sugarcane, flowers, and fruit trees, the smallest province in Argentina. It is in this oasis in the northwest corner of Argentina that Mercedes grows up with her older sister, Clara Rosa—also called Cocha—and her two brothers, Fernando and Orlando. The family resides in a poor, working-class area. The pink paint on the outer walls of their small, one-story house at Calle San Roque 344 is be-coming black from the soot and smoke of the nearby facto-ries, and in some places the paint is chipping off. The only light that gets into the house comes through two small win-dows with iron bars that face a narrow street where the chil-dren used to play, inventing their own games because they never had toys. Fortunately, they live close to the local park, which also has its ties to the date of Argentine independence, being named Parque de 9 Julio. It becomes a second home to them.

Growing up, Mercedes enjoys playing in the park with her siblings and the other children in their modest neigh-bourhood.[4] She is always cheerful and connects with others easily. But sometimes she prefers to be on her own and withdraws to her favorite tree. She likes to sit leaning against the bark while watching the insects buzzing around her. She is a robust child in many ways, but she also has a sensitive, reflective side that makes her wonder why some people are rich while others are poor. Very early in her life, she has a developed feeling for right and wrong. It is a sensibility caused directly by seeing her parents work so hard to keep hunger from their doorstep. Even doing their utmost, they often can't afford to buy food for their children. To distract their children from their hunger, they take them to the park to play every evening at dinnertime.[3] To Mercedes, Saturdays are the best days because that's when her father gets paid and the family can enjoy a meal of spaghetti with butter, the only hot meal they get all week. Often the hunger keeps her awake for hours at night.[4]

Still, later in life, Mercedes would come to say she had a happy childhood. "I do not wish to wail like someone who has lived in hunger, poverty, and cold. I lived my childhood in a poor house, which was however warmed up by the necessary feelings. My siblings and I always had the essentials, because we never lacked love. In this respect we were millionaires. Our parents not only sacrificed their lives, but they have been wise. They never put a burden on us for their sacrifices. They gave us everything they could, without revealing to us what they had to do to achieve this."[5]

Mercedes never truly grows out of the mindset of poverty she grew up with, and it shapes her social consciousness and gives her sympathy for the poor, which, along with the love of her parents, shapes her ideology and provides the firm foundation on which she will continue to stand. As an adult she concludes, "Poverty has always chased us, but it never broke us down. It only helped us to be free and choose our way of thinking."[3]

Mercedes has a close relationship with her grandparents. Her grandfather on her mother's side is half French, while her grandparents on her father's side are Amerindian with Quechuan roots, descending from the Inca empire. Mercedes is not aware of her Indian origins until her grandmother is dying and, in her delirium, starts speaking Quechua, but her new discovery instills in her a love for indigenous people and their culture, an affection that stays with her throughout her life.[2]

When Mercedes starts going to school, she quickly learns to read. She loves reading, and whenever it is time to cook at home, Ema orders Mercedes out of the kitchen and into her room where she can do so.[6] It is important to Ema that Mercedes gain as much knowledge as she can, and Mercedes never resists. She is curious and eager, and she absorbs the words of one book after another like a sponge. It broadens her horizons and gives her an understanding of history, culture, and people of different backgrounds from her own. Mercedes also sings and dances throughout her childhood. It is like walking and talking to her. Yet she remains shy and doesn't like to perform for others.

Then one day, in October 1950, when she is fifteen, her school music teacher, Josefina Pesce de Médici, discovers her ability to sing. To encourage Mercedes' talent, she asks her to lead the school choir in singing the national hymn at a school celebration. Mercedes tries to hide in the back, but Medici tells her to step up in front of all the teachers, her fellow students, and their parents, and to sing loud and clear. She is nervous, terrified, but she does so well that her teacher and some of her friends decide, without telling her, to sign her up for a contest at the local radio station. "I remember singing from the far end of my life. However, it is not the same to sing at home and for the world. There is a date for this. I was fifteen years old, and, one day, school finished two hours early. There was a competition on the town's radio station, LV12. I showed up more to play, rather than to sing."[5] Mercedes chooses to sing "Triste estoy" (I am Sad), a zamba by Margarita Palacios, under the pseudonym Gladys Osorio. She wins the contest, and the reward is a two-month contract with the radio station. This is the first stepping stone of her long career. Mercedes already knows that she wants to spend the rest of her life singing. A star has been born.

Her mother knows about the contest, but not Ernesto, her father, whom they know won't approve. He finds out any-way, having recognized his daughter's voice on the radio, and gets very upset. When Mercedes gets home, he slaps her in the face, which is something he has never done before. He doesn't want his daughter to become a singer because he thinks it will move her away from the family and lead to a wild and dissolute lifestyle. He doesn't believe there is any future in being a singer and wants his children to get an education so they can achieve more in life than he has. But to get the two months' contract with the radio station, Mercedes, a minor, needs her parents' signature, and Ema doesn't want to sign behind her husband's back. She is a clever woman who knows how to work on her husband, and, after a little persuasion, he finally gives in and signs the contract on the condition that Mercedes gets an education. To please him, she decides to become a dance teacher and study traditional Latin American dance, such as the Chacarera, Milonga, and Zamba.

The area where she grows up, with the influence of the indigenous culture of nearby Bolivia, inspires her to become a folk singer, although she could easily have made a career in opera instead and even considered it for a while. Her choice of education turns out to be an advantage for her career as an artist. But she can't stop singing and continues to get many invitations to perform at public events. Her parents have no choice but to get used to the idea, and, little by little, they do. Soon the whole family is following her wherever she goes.[4]

As much as Mercedes loves singing, and as often as she is doing so for audiences, it remains an immense challenge each time she stands up before them. She is still shy and, despite appearances, suffers from severe stage fright. It is a fear she knows she must overcome if she is ever to fulfill what is becoming her dream.

EMA AND Ernesto are interested in politics. They don't belong to any party, but they support Juan Perón, and even more so his wife, Evita, whom they admire for her outward beauty and her impact. Like them, Evita comes from a poor country region; unlike them (but perhaps like their daughter), she has worked her way out of poverty as an actress. Now, with her husband in office, she is responsible for the ministry of employment as well as the ministry of health. Her focus has been reforms to help the population's poorest, and she founds a charitable organization, Eva Peron Foundation, responsible for building houses, schools, hospitals, and homes for children. Evita is also behind the legislation that gives women the right to vote for the first time. She is a heroine in the eyes of the working class and is loved by millions of Argentines, even while society's right wing remains vehemently opposed to her.

At seventeen, Mercedes adores Evita and sees her as a real revolutionary. It is a major sorrow for her when, on July 26, 1952, Evita dies from cervical cancer, only thirty-three years old.[2]

IN 1957 Mercedes meets Manuel Oscar Matus, a composer and guitarist with a passion for traditional Latin American music, just like Mercedes. She falls head over heels for him and his songs despite the fact she is already engaged to someone else. "I was about to marry a rich man, but I married a poor man, and I never regretted it. That poor man was the author of the most beautiful songs I have been singing. If I hadn't married him, it would have been a big mistake."[3]

Oscar is also handsome and charming, with conclusive leftist ideals. They tie the knot on July 5, 1957. Mercedes doesn't want to leave Tucumán, where she has lived all of her life, but Oscar convinces her to move to Mendoza, in the central-west part of the country. The city is a cultural meeting point for artists, where many new beneficial friendships are forged. Mercedes soon becomes pregnant, and on December 20, 1958, she gives birth to a son, Fabián. Making a living from their music is a tremendous challenge; the young family struggles financially and lives in poor conditions that remind Mercedes of her childhood. Though they would love to stay in Mendoza, the looming circumstances force them to move to Buenos Aires, leaving friends and close relatives behind as they begin the journey toward securing better and more stable lives.[8]

But even in the capital, they soon find they are not able to make a living from their music alone, so they take cleaning jobs and work as night porters at hotels. Mercedes, like her parents before her, is suffering under the burden of not being able to feed her family. When she goes to the market, she buys the leftover ribs without meat on them–the bones can give some taste to the soup she cooks. For the first time in her life, she feels discouraged and depressed. This is not how she imagined life to be–not for herself or her son.

Artistically, Oscar Matus is a tremendous inspiration to Mercedes, and she finds great joy in singing his songs. He encourages her to dedicate herself even more to the original Latin American music traditions and to revive folk music, a genre that is about to be forgotten due to the onward march of contemporary music. He is the producer of her first two albums, *La voz de la zafra* (Voice of the Harvest) and *Canciónes con fundamento* (Songs with a Foundation). They often give concerts for the students at the campus of the University of Buenos Aires, where Mercedes receives considerable recognition from the students, who are impassioned by her voice and engaging personality. She always takes the time to talk with them and listen to their ideas. But at the same time, as her popularity increases, an artistic jealousy arises in Oscar and it taxes on their marriage. The financial pressure, still extant despite Mercedes' recent accomplishments, affects their marriage further. Regardless of her affection for Oscar's music, she is uncertain of the durability of their marriage. It seems that it is only their passion for music that keeps them together.

STARTING IN Chile under the influence of Violeta Parra and Víctor Jara, the New Song Movement (Nueva Canción Movimiento) spreads in the sixties and seventies all over Latin America. It is associated with revolutionary music because its musicians aim to unite with their listeners in a demand for democracy and social justice, hoping to achieve social and political change through music. The lyrics put issues such as poverty, imperialism, democracy, human rights, and religious freedom into the spotlight and relate to marginalized people by putting words to their struggles and their hopes. The song "Plegaria a un Labrador" (A Prayer to the Farmer), by Víctor Jara, for instance, deals with the need for agricultural reforms, giving farmers the right to own the land they cultivate.

Free us from the one who rules us in poverty.
Bring us your kingdom of justice and equality.
Blow, like wind, the flower of the ravine.
Clean, like fire, the cannon of my rifle.
Your will be done, finally, here on earth.
Give us your strength and your courage to fight.

Such ballads, loaded with political messages wrapped in evocative, poetic metaphors, are perceived as threats to oppressive governments. One of Mercedes' favorite songs, which in many ways becomes equivalent to her own struggle and resilience, is "Como la Cigarra" (Like the Cicada), by the Argentine poet and children's book writer María Elena Walsh.

I was killed so many times.
I died so many times
however, here I am
reviving.
I thank misfortune
and I thank the hand with the dagger
because it killed me so badly
that I went on singing
Singing in the sun
like the Cicada
after a year
under the earth
just like a survivor,
that's returning from war.

Mercedes Sosa and Oscar Matus are the key figures of the New Song Movement in Argentina. With a desire to exchange ideas with artists and movements throughout Latin America, they meet with eleven other artists and poets in Mendoza on February 11, 1963, to sign the New Song Movement (Manifiesto Fundacional de Nueva Canciónero). The movement emphasizes the continent's indigenous history and native cultural roots, making use of folk instruments like the Andean flute, the quena, pan pipes, and the ten-stringed charango.[9]

In Argentina, Mercedes and Oscar work closely with Armando Tejada Gómez, an Argentine poet living in Mendoza. Gomez writes the songs, Matus composes the music, and Mercedes Sosa provides the voice connecting the two. Mercedes never writes her own songs—her strength lies in interpreting the songs of others and making them her own. "I fall in love with a song like one falls in love with a man. I love what I sing,"[3] she says. She gets many of her songs from Víctor Jara and Violeta Parra of Chile. "Gracias a la vida" (Thanks to Life), by the latter of the two becomes one of the movement's best-known songs worldwide, thanks to Mercedes' interpretation, which is remarkably persuasive and personal, so much so that the song becomes her trademark for good. In the Unites States it is sung by Joan Baez, who also uses her popularity as a vehicle for social protest, expressing anti-imperialist views resulting from the Vietnam War.

OSCAR MATUS is a fervent communist and supports militant methods. Mercedes joins him in the party, but she can't accept its militant approach so she resigns shortly after. Despite the brevity of her membership in the Communist Party, she is pigeonholed the rest of her life as one of its members, stigmatized by right-wing politicians as communist and a threat. Meanwhile, the communists take advantage of her name appearing in their member lists, at the same time blaming her for not being a "real" communist because she doesn't break with the Catholic Church. However, Mercedes doesn't allow anyone to place her in a box. She is what she sings of in the song "Como un pájaro libre" (Like a Free Bird), a free bird who follows her heart and her conviction in everything she does.

Her involvement in the New Song Movement is an ideal platform where she can combine her art and her concern about human issues. She is a woman with a leftist ideology, but she doesn't see herself as a political leader and doesn't like being labelled as a protester either.[10] "Were they protesting songs? I've never liked that label. They were honest songs about the way things really are. I am a woman who sings, who tries to sing as well as possible with the best songs available. I was bestowed this role as a big protester, but it is not like that at all. I am just a thinking artist. Politics has always been an idealistic thing for me. I am a woman of the left, though I belong to no party and think artists should remain independent of all political parties. I believe in human rights. Injustice pains me, and I want to see real peace,"[11] she says.

By insisting on being an artist, she gets some enemies on the left, while her leftist ideology makes her an enemy of the right. It is a dilemma, but it doesn't stop her from taking a stand in her music. "Sometimes a song needs to have a social content. But the primordial issue is one of honesty. In Latin America, the mere act of an artist being honest is itself political,"[12] she says, and advocates that artists have the same rights to have an ideology as everybody else.

IT IS not only political dilemmas Mercedes has to overcome. She is also facing a moral dilemma; she has become pregnant for the second time. Mercedes loves children and wants more but feels it is irresponsible of her.[8] Her career is consuming almost all of her time and energy, and she is living a turbulent, often changing life that lacks the safe environment necessary to raise a child. She is already struggling to be the mother she wants to be to Fabián, and it is a huge challenge for her to reconcile her high expectations of herself as a mother with her ambitions as an artist. She is overwhelmed by the thought of having a second child, so when she becomes ill during her pregnancy, she decides to get an abortion, a decision that is hard on her and makes her feel that she is not able to live up to her ideals.[8]

This experience gives her a new understanding of young girls who have become pregnant against their will. She is not against the Catholic Church, but she sees it as a problem that the church is against teaching young adults about sexuality and fails to deal with the issue of children being molested by priests. Too many teenage girls die because they go to incompetent doctors who don't know how to do the procedure safely and correctly. She believes that the average fifteen-year-old girl is not able to take care of a child, and that such girls need someone to speak up for them.[8] As a result, she embarks on a lifelong journey, becoming a spokeswoman for women's rights, and, in 1995, she is honored for her work by receiving the UNIFEM Award from the United Nations.[13]

Mercedes never regrets her decision about getting an abortion, but she nonetheless feels guilt over it frequently.

THE FINANCIAL pressure, their unpredictable lifestyle, raising a child, their disagreements over politics, and Oscar's jealousy–which is causing him to mistreat her–is forcing her to question if she can keep her vows and stay in the marriage.[4] She is desperate to get out but is caught in a bind. She has always been a "good girl." She hadn't had sex with anyone before she got married, and she has never been unfaithful to her husband. According to the norms of the time and the traditional values of the area, she has grown up believing that good girls don't get divorced. Even so, she is considering another hard decision that goes against her values and her loyal personality. But while she's deliberating, she learns that Oscar has been unfaithful and wants to leave her for another woman. He makes the decision for her, easing her conscience. But she still feels humiliated and finds it hard to accept that he has abandoned her. Hatred is not a feeling she normally possesses, but Mercedes feels hatred toward the other woman for the rest of her life. "I did not leave the marriage. He abandoned me. A Tucumána girl marries for life. That destroyed me."[4]

Mercedes and Oscar have been married for eight years when Mercedes, thirty years of age, finally accepts that the marriage is leading to a dead end and consents to the breakup.

After the divorce, she feels heartbroken and lonely. She doesn't even have a permanent place to stay and moves from one small pension to another with Fabián, who is now seven. Eventually, she decides to send Fabián to live with her parents in Tucumán. Her income comes from singing at night-clubs in Buenos Aires, but she doesn't earn enough and has to get loans from some of her friends in order to survive. When the time comes to pay her friends back and she asks how much she owes, they all answer with variations of the rejoinder, "What money?" She is deeply moved by the sense of solidarity shown by her friends, who are artists struggling to make ends meet as well.

In 1965, Mercedes makes a significant step forward in her career. Thanks to the support of a very popular Argentine singer, Jorge Cafrune, who invites her to sing at the national folk festival in Cosquin, she gets a national breakthrough. At first, the festival committee doesn't want her to sing as they consider her a communist, but Jorge Cafrune insists. Standing on the stage with her arm around Fabián, who she brings along whenever she can, she gives her thanks to Jorge Cafrune and the committee for the opportunity to sing. The song that provides her biggest breakthrough is almost prophetic, its lyrics ominously pointing toward what she is about to face.

Night is coming to me in the middle of the afternoon,
But I don't want to turn into shadows,
I want to be light and stay.[4]

In 1967, a new life is taking shape. Professionally, Mercedes is being introduced on the big international stages. She gives concerts in Miami, Rome, Warsaw, Lisbon, Leningrad, and many other cities. She becomes engaged to Francisco Pocho Mazzitelli, her manager, whom she had developed a friendship with while still being married to Oscar. In the beginning, he was just a very good, supportive friend, but the friendship has grown into love. He becomes crucial for the way Mercedes develops as a musician, as he likes many different genres and introduces her to both classical music and jazz. Their relationship helps keep Mercedes from becoming further depressed and lonely after her divorce. Francisco, or Pocho as she calls him, pulls her out of the darkness and Mercedes realizes that she has to hold onto him to stay in the light.[4] They decide to get married in 1968. Pocho is a couple of years older than Mercedes, and he gives her the stability and peace she never experienced in her marriage with Oscar. He ends up being the love of her life, her true partner, and a substitute father for Fabián. He is also there supporting her through her grief when her father dies suddenly of a heart attack in June 1972, at the age of sixty-two.[8]

As THE popularity of the New Song Movement grows among the working class, it becomes a real threat to the ruling dictatorships across the continent. Soon many of its artists face political oppression—censorship, persecution, intimidation—and some are forced into exile. One of the leaders of the movement in Chile, Mercedes' good friend Víctor Jara, comes out in support of Salvador Allende for president. In 1970, Allende is inaugurated as the first socialist head of state in a Latin American country elected by democratic means.

When he steps out in front of the masses to be paid tribute for the first time, there is a banner hanging behind him that says, "It is not possible to have a revolution without singing."

Víctor Jara participates in all of Allende's political meetings. He gives free concerts in support of the government and tours all over the world, highlighting to the audience Chile's peaceful way to socialism. However, after a bloody coup on September 11, 1973, the military, led by the commander in chief Augusto Pinochet, removes Allende, who dies of unknown causes during the attack on the presidential palace.

At that same time, Jara is at the technical university in Santiago, where he is a teacher. The university lies only some hundred meters away from the presidential palace and is surrounded by the military, so no one can get out. Víctor calls his English wife, Joan, from the university and tells her to stay inside the house with their two girls until the fighting is over. He tells her he will spend the night at the university with other teachers and students and return home in the morning. They declare their love to each other before he hangs up. It is the last time she hears his voice. In the morning, the students and the teachers are attacked by the military, and, together with thousands of other pro-Allende Chileans, they are led to the national soccer stadium, Estadio Chile. Here Jara is tortured. First they force him to sing and play his guitar. Then they cut his hands off with an axe before killing him with forty-four shots in the head, chest, arms, and legs. A few days later, Joan finds his body in a ditch outside of Santiago.[14]

They did it out of fear. As one officer said, "Víctor Jara can make greater harm with his songs than one hundred machine guns." The officer's statement serves as an example of how powerful the New Song Movement has become and why the military junta under Pinochet bans the name and music of Jara all over Chile. Fortunately, his widow, Joan, manages to smuggle the majority of her husband's original music out of the country, allowing it to be copied and spread across the globe. His tragic death makes him a martyr, a symbol in the fight against fascism and social injustice in Latin America, and in the rest of the world.

When news of the assassination of Víctor Jara reaches Mercedes, she bursts into tears. Now she knows how far a regime may be willing to go in order to stop the singers of the New Song Movement. Simultaneously, she also realizes what a powerful weapon these songs are. She is determined to continue singing them no matter the cost, as long as they give hope to the people. Jara's death only adds fuel to the fire burning inside of her. Now, more than ever, she is ready to continue her resistance against the oppressors of the poor.

Mercedes' latest album, *Hasta la victoria* (Until Victory), contains songs with social and political content, clearly in response to these horrible events. The song "Plegaria a un labrador" is practically a red flag waved in the face of the bull-like right wing because the song is written by Jara. In Chile, the song has been censored. Meanwhile, in Argentina, the authorities under the leadership of Alejandro Agustín Lanusse feel similarly threatened and provoked by Mercedes' songs. Fearing she will incite a riot, they ban most of her songs, which cease to be played on the radio. Her records can no longer be sold in shops. She still has permission to perform if she keeps the banned songs off the program, but her freedom to express herself and make a living is heavily restricted. "I have always sung honest songs about love, about peace, about injustice. Unfortunately, some people feel threatened by the truth,"[15] she says.

The coup in Chile is a precursor for what will be a major blow to Mercedes. Argentina is going through one coup after another, which leads to political chaos and changing governments. Perón, who had been overthrown by a military coup in 1955 by Eduardo Lonardi, a Catholic nationalist, manages to come back into office in 1973, after years of exile in Spain. This fosters a small hope for democracy, but the Perónist party is divided between liberal and conservative factions, making it difficult if not impossible to govern. Perón has been strongly influenced by General Franco in Spain, and his new wife, Isabel, whom he has made vice president, is only interested in meeting the interests of right-wing groups. She is also preoccupied with the occult and has a close connection to the fortune teller José López Rega, whom she convinces her husband to employ as her private secretary. López Rega becomes responsible for setting up a paramilitary force, the Argentine Anticommunist Alliance, or Triple A, as it came to be known. Triple A is essentially mandated with the task of snuffing out all left-wing elements within the party.

Perón's last time in government is short, as he dies from a heart attack on July 1, 1974. Isabel Perón takes over after her husband dies and becomes the first non-royal female head of state in the western hemisphere. But she has hardly any political experience, much less ambition. She appoints López Rega as minister of social affairs and welfare. He is extremely fascist in his beliefs, and under his influence Isabel moves to the far right. She signs a decree that gives Triple A carte blanche to put down guerrilla activities and to "export all troublemakers." A death squad is organized, inspired by some of the thousands of Nazi war criminals Juan Domingo Perón allowed to enter Argentina after World War 2.[16] In 1974 they kill seventy left-wing opponents. The number grows fast, and in 1975 they murder fifty people per week![17]

During Isabel Perón's tenure as president, the country's economy falls into jeopardy. The peso falls by 70 percent, and the country experiences devastating inflation and a resulting recession. Concurrently, the opposition accuses her of taking enormous sums from the government's bailout package, the Cruzada de Solidaridad (Solidarity Crusade), and transferring them to her personal bank accounts in Spain. Hence she loses her last supporters, and in November 1974 she declares the country in a state of emergency.

MERCEDES FINDS herself in the middle of all this when, in 1974, she is invited by the Communist Party to Cuba. Her trip is viewed harshly by those in power, and a few days before she is supposed to leave, she receives a letter before a concert at Teatro Estrella in Buenos Aires. She opens it and freezes. Her heart pounds. Shivering, she reads the typed missive signed by Triple A telling her to leave the country within four days or accept the consequences.[4] She has a performance to complete and pulls herself together, pretending that everything is fine. But it bowls her over. Whatever she does, she knows her life and career are about to change forever.

After the concert, Pocho insists that they face their fear and walk back as they usually do instead of chicken out. But it is easier said than done. As they walk to Cordoba Street along Carlos Pellegrini Street in the center of Buenos Aires, they notice they are being tailed, an experience that leaves a lasting impression in Mercedes' memory. "It was a Saturday evening. I will never forget it. During this walk I learned what fear is," she says.[2]

They hurry back home, and, when they are safely inside, pull the curtains in the living room carefully aside to look down at the street. The same men are outside. They are standing on the pavement, peering up at the flat while taking a smoke. Mercedes begins to sweat. Her hands shake. Pocho puts his arm around her shoulders and tries to calm her, explaining that Triple A can't harm her because it would bring on too much international attention if they did. But Mercedes is convinced that her name figures on Triple A's list of "Dangerous Communists," even if it has been years since she was a member of the party. She also knows that they consider her songs treacherous. Mercedes is determined not to let anxiety and despair prevent her from singing. Somehow she gets used to having Triple A on her heels. She can cope because she remains gratified in her private life. Pocho helps her hold on.

Mercedes' suspicion that her name is on a list of archenemies of the state is proved right after her death. In 2013, the Argentine defense minister finds and releases secret records of the military junta's governing plan up to the year 2000 in the basement of the headquarters of the Argentine Air Force. The documents are signed by the general secretaries. Contained in the documents is a list of the names of 331 intellectuals, journalists, artists, and musicians who were blacklisted as being the most dangerous people to the regime because of their Marxist ideological background. The documents have legal value for the lawsuits that are still ongoing in Argentina.[18]

CHAOS AND political instability make way for another coup, and the military takes advantage of people's apprehension of communism, which is perceived as "the enemy within," and a threat to traditional Argentine and Western ideals. The task of the military becomes more than just protecting the outward borders of the country; they now also have to protect the ideological purity of the nation.

A military junta led by Admiral Emilio Massera, General Orland Ramón Agosti, and the previous military commander in the Argentine Army, Jorge Rafael Videla, successfully overthrows Isabel Perón on March 24, 1976. Two days later, Videla appoints himself president. This is not just another coup– Argentina soon faces the bloodiest and most shameful time in its history. Videla plans to eliminate everybody who opposes the regime. While he was still a military commander in the army, he gave an interview to a journalist at a conference in Uruguay and said that in order to guarantee national security, all the necessary would have to die. The reporter asked him to clarify who he was referring to, and Videla answered without hesitation, "Everybody who opposes the Argentine way of life."[17]

In most of the conservative media, the generals get positive coverage. They are described as doves who self-sacrificingly have taken on the burden of saving Argentina to avoid bloodshed. But shortly after their inauguration, the junta replaces the existing constitution with what they call el Proceso (the Process of National Reorganization). As if by magic, they give themselves the power to exercise all judicial, legislative, and executive powers. The generals appoint themselves protectors of the traditions, families, and property of the nation. Any critic of the new government is looked upon as opposition that has to be eradicated in order to protect the nation. Trade unions, political parties, and universities are subject to the control of the military. Both the police and the military get more authority. Communism has to be stopped at any cost. Across the country, 340 secret detention camps are financed by the state. Special military units are established for kidnappings, questioning, torture, and murder. No one feels safe. People are abducted from their homes at night by heavily armed men in civilian clothes. They go after pregnant women, children, babies, students, journalists, teachers, artists, nuns, priests, lawyers—anyone who shows any sign of sympathy with an enemy. As General Ibérico Saint-Jean, governor of Buenos Aires, says in 1977, "First we kill all the subversives. Then we kill their collaborators, their sympathizers, then those who are indifferent, and finally we will kill the timid."[17]

Armed squads raid people's homes and threaten entire families, blindfold them, handcuff them, and bring them to detention camps where they are systematically exposed to physical and psychological torture. Parents are forced to witness the torture of their children. Spouses are forced to witness each other being raped. It often happens in the presence of a doctor, who is responsible for keeping the victims alive as long as possible. When a victim dies they get rid of the body in order to remove evidence of their crimes.

Many families don't report someone missing for fear of inflicting more suffering to their missing relatives. When there is no body and a family member reports someone missing, the reporter risks being accused of the crime. In Rio de la Plata, unidentified bodies begin to wash ashore. It gets out that some of the torture victims are drugged, taken to an airport, boarded onto an airplane, and thrown out over the ocean—alive.

Referring to the assassinations as "disappearances," the generals try to refute any accusation of their involvement. "The disappeared are just that, disappeared. They are neither alive nor dead. They are disappeared," Videla says.

Many of the missing are children, abducted from their parents, including children who are born in captivity in the detention camps. (The women who give birth to them are often killed right after.) The regime takes these children and gives them to high-ranking officers in the military for adoption or, on some occasions, to innocent couples who don't know the origin of their child. The generals believe it is better for the children to grow up in a "respectable" family instead of being brought up by rebels. "Rebellious parents teach their children to rebel. It has to be stopped,"[17] General Ramòn Juan Camps, the chief of police in Buenos Aires, says in 1984 in an effort to justify his actions. The result of this policy is that many children grow up with a false history and a false identity, deprived of the rights that are internationally recognized as their universal human rights.

The relatives of the disappeared start to organize themselves in their search for their beloved. Azuenca Villaflor, a woman in her fifties who has lost her son and daughter-in-law, starts to meet with other mothers in her home to channel despair into action and to uncover what has happened to their children and grandchildren. In April 1977, fourteen mothers and grandmothers get together, aiming to expose the crimes of the regime to the world. They start to meet every Thursday at three thirty in the afternoon at Plaza de Mayo in front of the Government House, La Casa Rosada (The Pink House), in the heart of Buenos Aires. It is illegal to gather in public places, so instead they walk silently around, wearing white scarves symbolizing diapers and holding photos of their missing relatives. In October 1977, the Association of the Grandmothers of the Plaza de Mayo is established. Their mission is to find and reunite around 500 missing children with their families. They receive death threats and suffer insults and attacks by the army, but no one dies.

In order to stay under the radar, they meet in public places, pretending they are waiting for the bus or celebrating a birthday, when in fact they are making lists of the missing, with names and photos. They send these lists to organizations inside and outside of Argentina. They also gather proof that the children are still alive. They write letters to the supreme court, which always turns them down. Most judges refuse to take on missing-person cases, as they too are afraid to upset the regime and expose themselves and their families to danger. The judges who do dare receive death threats.

On Children's Day, August 5, 1978, one of the biggest newspapers in Buenos Aires takes a risk and prints a letter to the editor from the grandmothers in which they appeal to those who have adopted the children to bring them back. The letter causes a stir in Argentina as well as abroad. As a result, the grandmothers receive an anonymous tip about a missing child. To follow up, they begin working as detectives. Sometimes they will go to the hairdresser in the area where a missing child has been seen, for instance, or they apply to work as domestic helpers to get close to a certain family. In March 1980, they succeed for the first time in identifying two sisters who are found with a family in Chile. The family has no knowledge of the backstory of the adoption.

Having found the two sisters, the grandmothers face another challenge—they can't prove to the judge that these children really are missing relatives. Photos and locks of hair aren't enough because the Argentine courts aren't willing to do genetic tests. It forces the grandmothers to seek help from international scientists, who provides them with the proof they need.

Most of the grandmothers are Catholics, and they count on the church for support but are let down by the bishops, who tend to defend the political system. Even the pope, Paul IV, never answers the letter they write to him in 1978. So they change tactics and decide to get more international attention, writing 150 letters to embassies, newspapers, organizations, and politicians. In public they are called Las Locas de Plaza de Mayo (The crazy ones of Plaza de Mayo), but as they draw increasing international attention, they become a thorn in the side of the regime, especially when they are nominated for the Nobel Peace Prize, in 1980.[17]

AT THE onset of 1978, Mercedes receives devastating news about her good old friend Jorge Cafrune, who introduced her to the festival in Cosquin in 1965. He has returned to Argentina after having spent a couple of years in Spain and is giving concerts all over the country. The government has forbidden him to sing the controversial song "Zamba de mi Esperanza" (Zamba about my Hope), which he removes from his repertoire, but he also gives this fatal statement: "If my people ask me to sing it, I will sing it." As a consequence, Lieutenant Colonel Carlos Enrique Villanueva orders his execution, and on January 31 he is run over by a van driven by two nineteen-year-old boys. He dies from his injuries twelve hours later.

Two weeks later, Mercedes will face even more traumatic news that is going to affect her life permanently. The best thing that has happened to her is her relationship with Pocho. By now they have been together for ten years. It has been ten full years where they have worked and travelled to many different countries together. Mercedes has never had so much love in her life. With him by her side, she feels steady, strong, and resilient in the midst of all the political turmoil.

But the prophetic line from the song at her breakthrough in Cosquin, "Night is coming in the middle of the afternoon," is about to be fulfilled.

ONE DAY, Pocho arrives home early from work and goes straight to bed because he has a tremendous headache. Painkillers don't ease the pain. It only gets worse, and he is soon hospitalized. The examinations reveal he has a brain tumor. There is nothing the surgeons can do; it is too late. Everything happens so fast. He dies on February 22, 1978, after only a week in the hospital.

Mercedes still hasn't been able to process the news about the seriousness of the tumor and finds herself in a state of shock.

Pocho meant everything to her. Why him? Why so suddenly? They hardly had time for a goodbye. Mercedes is only forty-three years old and is already a widow. She has lost her best friend, her husband, and her manager. If it wasn't for her son, Fabián, she would want to die too. But Fabián is now an adult and very supportive during this crucial time. He makes sure she still has plenty of jobs, hoping that keeping her busy will take her focus away from the loss and that she will find a way out of her darkness.

SHORTLY AFTER Pocho's death, Mercedes is invited to give an aid concert for veterinarian students in the Argentine resort town of La Plata, south of Buenos Aires. Mercedes loves the students and their way of challenging the system. She sees them as the future and the hope of Argentina and is delighted to support them.

The university in La Plata is the leftist hotbed in the country, and it is under constant surveillance by the regime, something Mercedes is not concerned about when she enters the stage to applause. She is wearing a beautiful poncho of sky blue and white, the very colors of the Argentine flag. As the concert proceeds, she is carried away by the atmosphere of the place and doesn't hold back. From the audience, students ask her to sing "Cuando tenga la tierra" (When the Land Becomes Mine), which is about a new agricultural reform in favor of the peasants who have to pay rent to big estate owners in order to use the land they cultivate. The song has been banned, but Mercedes decides to give in to her audience. As she begins, heavily armed police and military forces abruptly rush in. Snipers are now pointing their guns at the stage and the audience. A young policeman jumps onstage and starts body-searching Mercedes, humiliating her. He touches her breasts, handcuffs her, and arrests her in front of her audience. When he is finished, he takes her hand and kisses it while whispering, "Forgive me, Dona Mercedes, but I was ordered to do this."[11]

Fabián has leapt to the stage to help his mother, but there is nothing he can do; he is arrested as well. Before Mercedes understands what is happening, she and her band have been detained along with the entire audience, 350 students. About the experience that is going to turn her life and career upside down, she would later say:

"I remember when they arrested me in front of my audience. I was singing at the university for the students who were studying to become veterinarians. It was their last year of their study. It had nothing to do with politics. I wasn't afraid. You can't sing if you are full of fear. But I felt humiliated and powerless. It is not possible to sing with a gun in your hand, and I am not out to kill anyone. I would rather be killed than have to kill someone. I can see that I probably was a bit naive at that time. I do not pretend that I was saintly in my attitude. Scheduling those shows was a way for us to push against the games of the dictatorship. I don't know why I thought I could win a struggle like that in a country in which so many people had been killed, but I tried. If Pocho had lived, he would never have allowed me to give that concert."[11]

Mercedes is charged preliminarily with civil disobedience. She is detained while the military humiliates her by asking her intimidating questions, threatening her, and forcing her to listen to her own songs. She spends eighteen hours in prison and is released due to international pressure and a bail of one thousand dollars. Once out of jail, she continues giving concerts, and tickets sell out fast, even if people are putting themselves at risk by showing up. Her concerts receive anonymous bomb threats and have to be cancelled, but she is still reluctant to the idea of leaving her country. "I can't live in any other place in the world beside this one, and whoever doesn't like my songs, they can leave," she says.[4] But eventually the military governor of Buenos Aires prohibits her from further performances, and Mercedes realizes that she can't continue her career in Argentina. If she wants to survive and keep singing, she has to flee the country. Therefore she decides to write a letter to her good friend José, in Paris, who has begged her to come:

Dear José,

With great emotion I received your letter on October 30, 1978. What happened to me was just dreadful. What a disgrace. After 18 hours I was released with my son,

Fabián. I will come to Paris in February. I need to breathe and let go of those resentments because they will do me great harm. I am going to stay as long as possible. They are cornering me here. I just returned from the theater. Some people had supportive words and others are wondering, "This idiot, why is she staying?" As if it were so easy abandoning one's people. Their embrace is what I will miss the most.[4]

Yours, Mercedes.

In theory, Mercedes can still enter and leave Argentina freely, as she hasn't been indicted on any charge, but she remains without permission to sing, which is a greater punishment for her. Persecuted and unable to make a living, she sees self-imposed exile as the only solution and decides to leave for France. It seems to be her only real way to flee from the darkness that has been creeping in on her. Since Pocho died, she has had thoughts of suicide. Exile is not only an escape from political persecution; it is also an escape from her own demons. Perhaps she can find peace from the sorrow tearing her apart when she is not singing.

Bottom left: Mercedes with Fabián, surrounded by her precious books. Mercedes was a thinking artist who believed that when she opened her mouth to sing everything inside her head came out too. Therefore it was important to her to read good books, watch good movies, and get inspiration from engaging with art.

Top Right: Singer Víctor Jara, who was tortured and murdered during the military dictatorship of General Augusto Pinochet. It took thirty-nine years before eight officers were sentenced for his murder. In 2003, Chile Stadium was renamed Víctor Jara Stadium.

Former Argentine President Isabel Peron next to her Minister of Social Welfare, Jose Lopez Rega, in Buenos Aires in 1975. In 1986, López Rega was arrested in the US and handed over to Argentina where he was accused of corruption, conspiracy, and homicide. He died of diabetes on June 9, 1989, in a prison in Buenos Aires while he was still waiting for his trial. Isabel Perón escaped to Spain, and the Spanish government still refuses to extradite her to Argentina.

Persecuted and unable to make a living, Mercedes sees self-imposed exile as her only way to flee from the darkness that has been creeping in on her.

Mercedes playing the traditional Argentine drum, la bombo.

Exile

ON FEBRUARY 2, 1979, Mercedes takes off to Europe with only a couple suitcases of personal belongings. Fabián travels with her to help her settle in. First they fly to Paris, where they meet with her French manager, Pierre Fatón, but she soon discovers how difficult it is to manage herself without speaking French. It leaves her helpless, and she concludes that it will be easier for her to settle down in Spain, where she has already accepted several invitations to perform. Consequently, she decides to move to Madrid, where she buys a five-bedroom house with the money she has earned on a marathon tour of eighty concerts in Brazil. She hopes that having a place on her own will make her feel more comfortable and at home, but when Fabián returns to Argentina and Mercedes is left by herself, she realizes how difficult it is to be alone on a foreign continent without any close relatives to turn to. The most significant people in her life used to be her family. Without them, she feels loneliness in a way she has never felt before. "Exile is a punishment, the worst kind of punishment. My son had helped me to Madrid via France and helped me buy a house. The day he left for Argentina I was left on my own, completely alone. The worst kind of loneliness you can imagine. I have experienced loneliness up close,"[2] she says. Later, she adds, "Exile has a fear of everything. It's permanent angst. The Greeks used to say the biggest punishment for a human being is exile. It's necessary to learn new customs, eat new foods, wait for letters that don't come and hold onto yourself to keep from going crazy."[19]

In Madrid, she is surrounded by people most of the time. Nevertheless, she still feels like a part of her has been amputated, especially when she returns at night and finds her big house empty. Then she gets the whisky bottle down from the shelf in her living room and starts drinking. After seven or so drinks, she feels better, but the relief is only brief.

She keeps the habit up for a couple of months before admitting its ill effects to herself and deciding to stop. Mercedes manages to discipline herself and never touches whisky again. For the rest of her life, she only orders one glass of wine when dining out.

She also tries to smoke hash. The first time it happens by mistake because she doesn't know what she has been offered until afterward. She likes it and tries it a second time, but once again she stops so she doesn't become addicted.[2] "Addiction is worse than prison," she says later. "I become sad when I see people ruined by drugs." There must be a better way to handle the loneliness without the use of alcohol or drugs, and she confides in her good friend Dr. Juan-David Nasio, who is a psychiatrist in France. He explains to her that loneliness often increases with popularity because a celebrity who is loved by many can't share his or her private struggles with the public.[4] Mercedes yearns for connectedness with people. She never pretends to be someone she is not, but she acknowledges that loneliness will most likely be her companion throughout life. She needs to find a way to cope with it. She must make friends with it, even though it doesn't happen overnight. But something else does.

ONE MORNING she wakes up and discovers that her voice is almost gone–she can barely whisper. She hasn't got a cold, and she is anxious that it is something serious. Straightaway she rushes to see a specialist, who examines her thoroughly. It is a rare phenomenon and he can't detect the source but suggests that the stress she has been exposed to has made her gastric acid rise.[20] He advises her to use antacids to keep the gastric acid from affecting her vocal chords. He also tells her to protect her voice and not exert pressure to it. All she can do is wait and hope to recover. She cancels her forthcoming engagements, which gives her plenty of time to ponder. If it isn't a physical problem, what is it then? Can it be a somatic condition? Is her outer voice reacting to the pain of having the power of her voice taken from her in Argentina?

Now that she is forced to slow down a little, she pays more attention to her inner voice. She understands that she has become ill because she has avoided dealing with her painful memories. Denial has been a defense mechanism protecting her from facing the pain.

"It was a mental problem, a problem of morale. It wasn't my throat, or anything physical. When you are in exile, you take your suitcase, but there are things that don't fit. There are things in your mind, like colors and smells and childhood attitudes, and there is also the pain and the death you saw. You shouldn't deny those things because to do so can make you ill."[11]

In an interview for the recording of *Cantora* in 2009, she elaborated that her private doctor years later explained to her that she had suffered from a masked depression,[3] a condition where the physical symptoms of depression are present but not the psychological ones.

THROUGHOUT HER exile, she is compelled to deal with her stage fright too. Even though she doesn't stand stiff as a totem pole in front of her audience as she did in her early career, she prefers to sing with her eyes closed as a way to cope. "My shyness is so strong that it truly causes stomachaches because I have to stand onstage and pretend to have confidence, which I don't,"[4] she reveals.

Repeatedly she performs for a non-Spanish speaking audience. To keep their attention, she must look at them to maintain the contact. It forces her to change her performance style. Instead of letting fear limit her career, she moves out of her comfort zone and trains herself to look directly at her audience, in spite of what her insecurity whispers to her. To interact with people rather than shutting them out makes her a much more powerful performer.

Her time in Europe gives her the opportunity to expand her musical horizons and enlarge her career. In 1988, she says in an interview with Larry Rohter, at *The New York Times*, what a landmark the exile became to her career. "By distancing me from my homeland and ripping me out by my roots, it forced my repertoire to become more international. Before, I was always tied to our rhythms and our songs. I wouldn't be able to do the things I am doing now, recording with jazz groups and orchestras, if I had not made a path for myself outside of Argentina. As bitter as my experience of exile was, it made me grow and mature as an artist because it opened new horizons."[11]

Invitations are running in from all over Europe, and the audiences in Europe are captivated by the small woman with the striking voice and enchanting entity. She often performs wearing her black and red poncho, emphasizing her identification with her Indian roots. She brings along her big traditional Argentine drum, la bombo, which is made of wood and sheepskin and on which she plays energetically. She likes to use the bombo because it has the booming sound of a heartbeat, which is important to her music.

"Gracias a la vida" and "Sólo le pido a Dios," is a permanent part of her program during the exile, and she receives her loudest ovations whenever she sings it. The latter is a world anthem for peace, written in 1978 by acclaimed songwriter León Gieco. "Mercedes wants León to see the impression his song has on people and decides to call him. León recalls her saying, "Hi baby. I'm in Frankfurt. Catch a plane tomorrow and come."[3]

León manages to show up at her next concert. Mercedes drags him up onstage, where he plays his guitar and his mouth organ, singing along with her. The audience explodes in applause. For a brief moment, in León's company, Mercedes doesn't feel lonely.

IN 1979, her career reaches another height. She participates in the first Amnesty International concert, in London, and she also receives an invitation to perform at the Royal Festival Hall. Twenty years later, she will be standing on the same stage while the Chilean dictator, General Augusto Pinochet, under house arrest in London, is sentenced for his crimes against the Chilean people. One of the most emotional moments in Mercedes' life is on that stage in October 1999, as, with a tearful voice, she shouts to her audience, "I cannot believe I am in London singing these songs, with Pinochet under house arrest."[21] She then proceeds to sing her most emotional version to date of "Todo cambia" (Everything Changes).

During the three years she spends in exile, Mercedes becomes one of the world's most esteemed international singers, as she often travels outside of Europe. She receives invitations from Israel, Canada, Columbia, and Brazil. Both Columbia and Brazil offer her permanent citizenship, but her love for Argentina keeps her from accepting. Every time she is in an airport and sees a plane from the Argentine airlines, Aerolineas, she has to look away to withhold her tears.[7] Being reminded of home "makes her bleed a volcano," as the metaphor says in the song, "País" (Country),

Her love of her home country grows substantially during the separation. As Mercedes would say about the song, "Serenata para la tierra de uno" (The Song for One's Own Country), "I was deeply moved by the song 'Serenata para la tierra de uno' because it puts into words the pain of being far away from home. I had to leave my country. But the further away from home you get, the closer it is to your heart."[22]

Consistently she uses her new European platform, her concerts, and all the related interviews to bring attention to human rights violations in many parts of Latin America. Her fight against tyranny and oppression is not over.

She spends three years in exile but feels desperate and can't wait to get back. Consequently, she decides to return to Argentina, even if the regime is still in power and she doesn't have any guarantee that they will let her in. Her heart is beating rapidly and her eyes are smarting from holding back her tears as she boards the aircraft to Buenos Aires in February 1982. But she remains hopeful and looks forward to seeing her family and friends. As the plane takes off, she releases years of constrained homesickness with silent tears.

Mercedes hardly manages to get any sleep on the long journey. Thoughts are spinning in her head; impressions from the last three years keep popping up. She remembers all the different airports she has been in. She thinks of the new friendships she has made and about how all the unexpected changes in her life have pushed her forward, requiring her to develop, not just as an artist but as a person as well. Reluctantly she admits that exile, as tough as it has been, has become a gift in disguise. The thought soothes her for a while, but when the plane is preparing for landing, she starts to worry about what will happen when she gets out. Where will she go if they don't let her into the country? And her fellow countrymen—will they still remember her? Her music has remained banned during her time away.

She feels at home as soon as she steps outside and senses the warm summer air touching the skin of her face. She moves slowly toward passport control. The police officer at the counter recognizes her immediately and takes his time looking through her passport and all its European stamps. He eyes her with an arrogant expression while he tells her that she is not allowed to enter the country. Being so close to home, Mercedes decides to stand up for herself. She gathers all the dignity and authority she can come up with and replies, "I am a citizen in this country, and I have a right to enter."[3] The officer, seemingly unprepared for the confidence with which she speaks, simply places a stamp in her passport and lets her pass. Mercedes knows that it won't take long before the news of her arrival reaches the regime and she will be put under surveillance again, but all she can think of right now is getting to the arrival hall. All she wants is to see her family again.

As she drives out of the airport, Mercedes is in for the surprise of her life. People have gathered all along the road waving banners that say "Welcome back to your home country, beloved Negra."[23] The car drives slowly through the streets, and a procession of horse-riding men in Gaucho outfits, the traditional clothing used by the cowboys in Argentina, follows the car. As the procession reaches the city center of Buenos Aires, people flock around the car so it can barely maneuver any further. Mercedes smiles and waves to them through the closed window while photographers with their enormous lenses preserve the moment. All worries of whether anyone would still remember her are put to rest. Her people welcome her as a national heroine.

Mercedes knows that with such a welcome comes tremendous responsibility. She cannot disappoint her people; they still need her. The military is still in power; the Dirty War isn't over. The generals' grip might be loosening, but they are still in control. Mercedes' voice, emerging from silence, must now be louder than ever.

"Kicking me out was a big mistake because they let loose around the world a famous artist, and in Europe the press was already against them. And then it was also a mistake to let me come back when they were still in power. That is how they were, arrogant. Returning was a way for me becoming strong and secure again."[4]

Having become a symbol of democracy in people's minds, her songs are going to be more convincing and powerful than ever before. She is determined to once again use her music on behalf of those who suffer from poverty and injustice. Mercedes wants to earn her title of the Voice of the Voiceless. She will never again be silenced by fear:

"If the singer is silenced, life ends
For life itself is a song
If the singer is silenced by fear
All hope, light and joy dies."
"Si se calla el cantor," by Horacio Guarany

Mercedes and León Gieco at a press conference. León Gieco had also fled from Argentina during the Dirty War when he received death threats after singing at a demonstration protesting the closure of the university of Buenos Aires. He lived in exile in California when Mercedes asked him to join her in Germany.

Mercedes Sosa in her home province, Tucumán.

Mercedes Sosa and León Gieco

Time after Exile

S OON AFTER HER homecoming, Mercedes plans to conduct thirteen concerts in seven days in the opera house, Teatro Ópera, in Buenos Aires. She thinks the international attention she gets will keep the military from harming her, since they want to avoid drawing attention from outside. Still, there are risks, if not to her, then to the fans who show up in the sold-out theater. The police will be present, Mercedes knows. As she later admitted, "It was in 1982, just before the war about Falkland Islands. It was a bit insane, but I planned thirteen concerts in seven days. At that time the military was still in power, and everybody knew what could happen."[2]

On February 17, the day before she gets onstage in Argentina for the first time in three years, Mercedes has an inner conflict. Something she has long pushed aside keeps popping up whenever she looks in the mirror. The person who looks back is a stranger, one she finds it difficult to accept. What happened to the slim and athletic young woman she once was? Mercedes has been hiding her weight from herself and others by wearing the ponchos, but that won't be enough anymore, and she is concerned about the reaction from her audience. She knows what attracts people: you must be blonde, tall, blue eyed, and definitely lacking Indian traits. Mercedes is just the opposite. She is small, overweight, brunette, and very indigenous in her features. Her normal confidence is replaced with a temporary feeling of inferiority, feeling uncertain about how the audience will respond to her. She admits to herself that it is quite the paradox that on the one hand she is ready to fight the regime at the risk of her life, and on the other hand she worries about what people will think of her appearance. It reminds her that even though she is admired and a role model to many, she is just as human as everybody else and mustn't expect herself to be infallible. "I'm a bunch of holy things mixed with human stuff. How can I explain – Worldy things."

Her weight problem follows her for the rest of her life, but the anxiety over her audience's reaction is soon extinguished. Just before entering the concert hall on February 18, 1982, the atmosphere is quivering with excitement. People are cheering, yelling, and clapping even before she reaches the microphone. Mindfully she stands still before the crowd, closes her eyes, breathes deeply, and takes in the moment. For almost a minute she just stands there in a meditative silence before breaking out with the symbolic song, "Como la cigarra" (Like a Cicada). Loud and clear, she proclaims that she is back; she is still standing and still singing.

The audience is ecstatic. After the first few stunning stanzas, it is obvious that they are in front of a musical genius. With her smooth alto voice—sonorous, compelling, emotionally charged, and impassioned—she casts a spell over her listeners. She is undoubtedly a more forceful artist than she used to be. If the response from the audience is an expression of people's will for change, the generals have every reason to be shaking. Mercedes seems able to start a revolution with her voice alone. She is planting seeds of freedom and justice in her listeners' minds, not only with her songs, but by her example of courage as well. All their pent-up fear and pain from living with persecution finds language when she sings. As she has said, "In my voice sings neither you nor I, but Latin America."[24]

At one of the thirteen concerts, Mercedes decides to sing "La carta," by Violeta Parra, a banned song describing the conditions of people in Chile. As soon as she starts, a large number of policemen get up and order that she stop, to the cries of those in the concert hall. The police give warning that they will send everybody home if she sings that song again. Afterward, the concert organizer and Fabián come up to her, their faces pale with concern, and plead with her to take the song out of her repertoire.[2]

The highlights of the thirteen concerts are recorded and released with the title *Live in Argentina* and sell hundreds of thousands of copies. A critic at *Esquire* describes the album like this:

"Her voice nearly strikes you dead. It is soft, deep, and compelling. And it moves you as it did the thousands of adoring countrymen who could be heard erupting into applause."

After she's finished, Mercedes is forced by the Generals to return to Spain, where she still has her house, but by mid-year she travels back to Latin America for good and introduces her new record, *Gente humilde* (Humble People).

DURING THE first five years of the dictatorship, the working class has been dormant, but Mercedes' return to Argentina raises their hope that democracy is still possible. In

April 1982, two months after her concert series, the country is undergoing a devastating economic crisis that sparks civil resistance against the military. The generals decide to demonstrate their power by reclaiming sovereignty of the Falkland Islands, which has been ruled by Great Britain for a hundred and fifty years. By invading the islands, they hope to distract attention from the economic crisis and to win back public favor by winning. The first Argentine troops reach the Falkland Islands on April 2, 1982, after the negotiations about the sovereignty between Great Britain and Argentina fail. It turns out to be a fatal decision. Margaret Thatcher also needs to win a war and fights back in a way the generals never expected. They also don't get the backup from Ronald Reagan they had anticipated. To the contrary, Reagan imposes economic sanctions on Argentina and equips the Brits with all the technology they need in order to trace the movements of the Argentine troops.[24] On July 14, the Argentines surrender, and the war is officially over the day after.

The unexpected loss of the war is the final blow to the regime. By now the truth about their involvement in the kidnappings and disappearances has been exposed to the public. Many people have nerved themselves to reveal their tragic stories, which cause waves of protests from the civilian population against the government. In October 1982, human rights groups organize a national March for Life. More than ten thousand people turn up in spite of the government's prohibition. In April 1983, foreseeing their downfall, the junta publishes a document in which they defend their acts in the war against rebels and terrorists. It is a document that contorts seven years of history and triggers much national and international anger. Another demonstration follows in July

1983, this time with more than fifty thousand people in attendance.

ARGENTINA'S MILITARY regime will soon be transmitted to the trash can of history. Fifty thousand people are gathered at the soccer stadium Ferro Carril del Oeste in Buenos Aires to celebrate the coming of democracy. Mercedes is excited. Triumphantly she conquers the stage with an imposing presence that captivates the audience. It is a warm summer evening. Some men have taken off their T-shirts and use them as banners. Men are dancing with children and girlfriends on their backs and shoulders. The audience radiates exhilaration. They jump and dance and clap with their arms lifted high. Mercedes has never performed for such a large crowd before, and she has a feeling that this concert will go down in history. Before she opens her mouth to sing, she stands still in front of her audience for a long time, gazing tenderly at them as she receives their tribute. A gentle summer breeze is playing with her hair, and she realizes the nightmare is over. Then she sets out with, "Guitarra enlunarada," and as an echo, the crowd roars back at her, shouting, "Libertad, libertad, libertad!"[25] (Freedom).

Following the first song, she introduces her four-piece band, the same musicians she used before her exile and who have become like family to her: Nicolás Brizuela on guitar, Gustavo Spatocco on keyboards, Rubén Lobo on drums, and Carlos Genoni on bass—they are all eminent performers now themselves.

Mercedes has extended her repertoire to feature a couple of rock songs, and one of the major surprises she has for her audience is that she has invited Charly García, the biggest rock star in the Spanish-speaking world. He enters the stage from a side entrance and passes the band as he walks across to Mercedes, who stretches out her arms to embrace him. Having hugged and kissed, he sits by the piano and starts playing the song "Inconsciente colectivo" (Collective Unconsciousness). Charly is a musical genius who began composing on piano when he was only three years old. At the age of twelve, he was a trained music professor. During the dictatorship, he became known for getting close to the line without overstepping it by writing ambiguous lyrics, and he managed not to get his songs banned. The text of "Encuentro con el diablo" (Meeting with the Devil), for example, refers to the minister of security, Albano Harguindeguy, who requested that all critical artists leave the country or turn down their criticism of the political conditions.

The concert reaches its climax when Mercedes starts singing "Todo cambia" (Everything Changes). She holds the microphone toward the audience, which sings back at each refrain, "Cambia todo cambia." Everything changes, except, that is, the love of one's country:

"*What changed yesterday*
will have to change tomorrow
Just as I change in this foreign land
But my love doesn't change
no matter how far away I find myself
neither the memory nor the pain
of my country and my people."

"Todo cambia," by Julio Numhauser Navarro

The emotional song peaks when Mercedes takes off her long scarf and begins to dance. Swinging the scarf above her head she moves about the stage with agility and grace, her face radiating when she looks directly at the audience. It surely is a far more outgoing person who has come back from exile. She is extraordinarily expressive and acts her songs out with vivid gestures—even her voice has changed, becoming deeper and richer when she whispers a love song, more dynamic when she calls out for battle. Mercedes describes her change and what caused it:

"My songs used to be very introvert. Now it is a song that goes out from me. When an artist meets opposition, his power rises, and what does the artist do? He grows. Music must develop, so must the artist."[2]

During the entire concert, she is like a volcano belching love toward the people, who continually return it. A man in the front row throws his sweaty worker's cap up to her onstage. She grabs it, holds it between her hands before gently kissing it, and hands it back to him. Another person passes her a long-stemmed red rose, which she receives with a devoted look, saying, "Gracias." This communication between Mercedes and her audience all happens while she keeps on singing. Her altruistic personality is outstanding, and it is striking how many hugs she gives out onstage. When fellow artists join her, she gets up and spreads her arms to embrace them as soon as she sees them. Being shorter than most, she often leans toward the colleague next to her with her arm around his or her back when they are singing a duet. Her musicians also get pats on the head or shoulder when she moves past them. The entire concert shows that she "sings for people because she loves them," as she always points out.[25]

Symbolically, she finishes the concert with the song that once got her arrested, "Cuando tengo la tierra" (When the Land Becomes Mine). This time no one will stop her, and she walks back and forth at a high, determined speed. With outstretched arm and clenched fist, she shouts, "Campesino" (Peasant). Someone throws the Argentine flag up on the tribune, and Mercedes catches it decisively and waves it above her head while the audience celebrates.

The concert marks the shift to democracy. By the end of 1983, an album as well as a movie recorded at the concert is released with the name *Como un pájaro libre* (As a Free Bird).

THE FIRST democratic election after the fall of the military junta is won by Raúl Alfonsin, from the Radical Party, with 51 percent of the vote. Alfonsin has long been in opposition to Juan Domingo Perón and the military dictatorship, and in his election campaign he promised not to compromise on human rights. He also promised to cancel The Law of National Pacification—a law the military junta had made in order to give amnesty to army personnel for their crimes. Mercedes doesn't take the new democracy for granted and is eager to support it. Therefore, she gives Raúl Alfonsin her full endorsement and backs him up with her presence at public events. "It would be a betrayal of everything I believe in and represent to stay away from what is going on. We have a democracy now, one that is fragile and still anguished, but fortunately, it exists. It is a great exercise in which all of us, whether we are artists or military, must collaborate if we are to keep democracy on its feet and walking,"[25] she says.

On December 10, 1983, Alfonsin is inaugurated as the new president, and the first thing he does is nullify pacification laws, just as he promised. He appoints the Argentine National Commission of the Disappeared (CONADEP) to investigate all the cases of the missing Argentines and bring charges against the guilty. After nine months, the commission publishes a fifty-thousand-page report based on witness statements. The report is named *Nunca Más* (Never Again), and sells two hundred thousand copies in a few weeks. It estimates that approximately nine thousand people have gone missing, but in reality the number is more likely around thirty thousand because many of the kidnappings were never recorded.[17]

Alfonsin puts nine of the highest ranking officers from the past three juntas before a military court. This is a big mistake. The trial turns into a farce as the military court doesn't want to pass judgment on its own. As a result, in April 1985, the accused are placed before a civilian court instead. This time they are charged with 711 counts of murder, illegal detention, torture, rape, and robbery. Five of the nine generals are sentenced to prison, for terms ranging from four and a half years to life. The verdict leads to increased tension between the government and the military, and members of CONADEP are exposed to bomb threats in their homes and offices by sympathizers of the dictatorship.[17]

In order to keep a lid on the threats from the military, Alfonsin implements a law on December 24, 1986, called

Punto Final (Full Stop Law). The law gives the prosecutors sixty days to bring their accusations, after which the chapter is considered closed and no one can bring further charges to court. Hundreds of officers are brought to trial during this period, and the military threats against the government increase. People are demonstrating in the streets on behalf of their democratically elected government. But Alfonsin later has to leave office due to economic problems and hyperinflation. This makes way for the Perónist Carlos Menem, who wins the next election with 47 percent of the vote in May 1989. In his election campaign, he promises to improve the conditions for the working class, but during his presidency, he does the exact opposite: he cuts down on the bailout packets to the poor. He also gives amnesty to many of the convicted felons Raúl Alfonsin arrested. Even Isabel Perón is released and pardoned. She had been under house arrest for five years for the forced disappearances and for crimes related to her issuance of the 6 October 1975 decree calling for the armed forces to "annihilate subversive elements" during her presidency.

The Argentine people feel abused again. They want the truth about the dictatorship revealed, but instead the aggression, threats, and persecutions of critical journalists under Menem's presidency intensifies. On November 11, 1993, the first journalist in the new democracy, Mario Bonino, disappears while he distributes flyers informing the public about attacks on journalists. A few days later his body is found in a river, but no one is held responsible. As thousands of Argentines gather in protest at Plaza del Mayo, Mercedes Sosa shows her support by entering the stage to sing "Honrar la vida" (Honor to Life).

THE GRANDMOTHERS of the Plaza de Mayo continue their search for their missing grandchildren after the Dirty War is over. When CONADEP in 1983 orders the excavation of hundreds of mass graves, they react to the unprofessional way it is carried out by the Argentine scientists. The bones are randomly piled next to the open graves, making genetic testing and identification impossible. Hastily they set up a meeting with CONADEP and urge them to cooperate with scientists at the American Association for the Advancement of Science (AAAS), which sends a delegation of forensic scientists to assist in the exhumations.

In 1986, they meet with President Alfonsin, who agrees to make a genetic data bank that can be used by the relatives of missing children until 2050. Concurrently he implements a new law implying that adoptive parents who refuse to be tested will be considered coconspirators in the kidnappings. For the first time in history, forensic science is used for humanitarian causes. Based on the DNA testing of their grandparents, missing children can get empirical evidence and trace their original families with 99.9 percent certainty.

Most of the grandmothers are merely housewives who rarely leave their homes without their husbands. But they transform themselves through their personal losses, establish the National Genetic Data Bank, and influence international legislation on adoption by helping to formulate the content of the United Nations Convention on the Right of the Child, which is ratified by 191 countries. It gives adopted children the right to know that they are adopted and gives them full access to their journals when they turn eighteen. The Grandmothers of the Plaza de Mayo have made it possible for adopted children all over the world to get to know their roots and their true identity.[17] By December 2017, one hundred and twenty-seven children stolen by the junta have been reunited with their families.[26]

Mercedes respects the grandmothers' work and continues to support them. She understands the importance of knowing one's roots and one's history.[28] Furthermore, the grandmothers' accomplishments confirm her conviction that, "It is important to react to this world and not leave it up to others and to the politicians to make the world a better place for everyone. I think it is a huge mistake to believe that the big changes shall come from political parties. No, they have to come from each of us."

In 1991, Mercedes dedicates a memorial concert at the Ferro Carril del Oeste Stadium to the Grandmothers of the Plaza de Mayo.[28]

MERCEDES HAS earned good money over the years and will never again face the poverty she experienced in her childhood or as a young artist. She will never lack anything for the rest of her life, nor will her family. She can afford to buy a luxurious place for herself, but she prefers to live in her big flat on 9 Julio Avenida, opposite the magnificent building hosting the French Embassy, in the center of Buenos Aires. There is little that is pretentious about her lifestyle; becoming well-off doesn't make her superficial. "I don't give a hoot about owning an airplane or a swimming pool. I just want to live in peace,"[28] she says.

Her view on inequality in society doesn't change either. She is still advocating that everyone must have a home with a bed to sleep in and a job to provide for themselves. "I have the dream that every person must have food to eat, clothes to wear, and a house to live in. That suffering must end, and that the worker can be proud of his labor and proud of being a worker. The most compassionate way to help the poor is by giving them a job, so they can provide for themselves," she says.[2] With her earnings, she supports the immigrants from Peru, Bolivia, and Paraguay who live illegally in an area of Buenos Aires called Bajo Flores. She donates money for a new transmitter at their little radio station, which transmits directly to the immigrants, and she also supports their soup kitchen. She provides cloth and sewing machines to some of the ladies in Bajo Flores and invests in a ravioli factory.[2] Her practical approach is rewarded. In 1992, she is declared a citizen of honor by Buenos Aires for her social engagement.[13]

JUST AS her sympathy with the poor hasn't changed, neither has her affection for indigenous people. Even though she receives invitations to perform in all of the most prestigious places in the world, there is a voice inside her reminding her of her Indian roots. She wants to reach out to the native people who might not know who she is or who can't afford to attend her concerts. She feels that until she has made such a connection something important is missing.

One day she is interviewed by a journalist who tells her that he has been in contact with some of the native Argentines and has asked them if they know Mercedes Sosa. They answered, "We have never met Mercedes Sosa, but we know her songs and we know that she is one of our own."[2] This feedback makes her proud and motivates her to make a concert tour to the remote areas of Argentina and to perform for free in order to make contact with the natives.

The tour takes her first to Bolivia, then to La Quiaca and Jujuy in the northwestern part of Argentina, three hundred kilometers north of her hometown, San Miguel de Tucumán.[27] In this part of the country, most people know her already, and she gets a special warm welcome. At a petrol station in the outskirts of town, a group of children recognize the tour bus and run toward it. Eyeing Mercedes, they throw their arms around her and kiss her. "I am so thankful for the love of the people. Even the children who don't understand what I sing about love me,"[25] she comments as she thinks about the experience.

Sometimes they make a stop in a small village on the way to have a break, meet with people, and take a look around. Mercedes feels at home when she takes a walk in the narrow alleys between the plain, whitewashed houses. Wearing her poncho and her hair up in a ponytail, she blends in well with the locals. Some of the adults come up to greet and kiss her. Shy, ruddy-faced children with wispy hair follow her curiously wherever she goes. Sometimes she sits down spontaneously on a stone step with her big drum and starts singing them the lullaby "Duerme negrito" (Go to Sleep Little Girl).[25]

Driving all the way from the north of Argentina, passing through Patagonia, they travel more than four thousand kilometers before reaching the southernmost city in the world, Ushuaia. In this cold, windy subpolar location, she finishes the tour entertaining and making friends with the Fuegians, the native people of Tierre del Fuego, who live in more poverty than she has seen anywhere else on her tour. Again it is the children who get Mercedes' attention. And when she sees how they have invented their own toys and use old boxes for sledding down the hills, she is reminded of her own childhood and how she used to play with her homemade toys in the park. Mercedes knows that many of these children will never have a chance to get out of poverty, and it leaves her further determined to make a difference for the children in Latin America.

In 1999, when given the chance by UNICEF to become their Goodwill Ambassador for the children of Latin America and the Caribbean, she accepts promptly. Without hesitation, she dedicates herself to the task for the rest of her life. When asked in an interview about which achievement in her life makes her most proud, she answers, "That I became a UNICEF ambassador and spoke up for the children in Latin America and the Caribbean. A childhood in suffering creates desperate men and women"[6]

NOW IN her early fifties, she hopes that she can pass something positive on to the younger generation, especially the young artists. "I have a great deal of respect for the young, for those who question and challenge things and always have. I want to give the young people a very important message that the world matters to them,"[11] she says. "The military dictatorship in my country paralyzed people. Today a new generation is coming alive, filled with young songwriters experiencing the passion of their freedom."[15]

One of the ways she encourages the young generation is by bringing them along to some of the big music festivals that take place every year in different countries in Latin America. The biggest is the festival in Cosquin in the province of Cordoba. It spans over nine days at the end of January. It was here Mercedes had her breakthrough in 1965, and, excepting her years in exile, she has participated ever since. Just as she had been introduced by Jorge Cafrune then, she is now keen on promoting the younger generation of artists herself, and invites many lesser-known ones to sing with her onstage. Many have their breakthroughs as Mercedes brings them into the spotlight and uses her prestige to introduce them to new audiences. She is never afraid of sharing her fame, and she thinks that many of the artists sing far better than she. The young artists, for their part, admire her. She becomes sort of a godmother who pays attention to their work and gives them her blessing.

One of the artists she often invites onstage with her is the Argentine composer and singer Víctor Heredia. "Mercedes forced me to sing at every concert, and she forced people to listen to me. I always call her Mummy because she is my second mother,"[3] Heredia reveals about how he got his breakthrough. He has written the song "Todavía cantamos" (We Still Sing), which after the downfall of the regime becomes a regular part of Mercedes' program.

"We still sing, still ask,
still dream, still hope,
in spite of our wounds
caused to our lives by the spirit of hatred
that exiled in oblivion our beloved."

Spending time with the young people and listening to their music keeps her current and informed about genres other than her own. Instead of playing it safe, she has the courage to cross stylistic boundaries and adds Argentine tango, Cuban Nueva Trova, Brazilian Bossa Nova, and jazz and rock influences to her repertoire. "My career has been a continual search not for applause but a personal musical quest involving change, taking chances. I didn't abandon folk music, but I began singing some of the jazz-inflected compositions in Portuguese by Milton Nascimento, Chico Buarque, and other Brazilian pop masters. I'm still experimenting, searching. I don't feel old; I am an artist who is constantly changing her repertoire,"[28] she says.

Just as she builds a bridge between generations, she also uses her fame to build a bridge between music genres that used to be far from each other. She remains faithful to folk music and to her "New Song" roots, however, and she inspires young artists to keep traditional folk music alive as well. Whatever she does, she never sells out her political opinions, and she still sings the songs of protest. But progressively, more songs are added to her repertoire that don't necessarily have political content. More love songs are added, for instance, "Tonada del viejo amor" (Tune of Old Love) and "Insensatez" (Senseless). No matter which genre she sets out to sing, her solidarity with people who suffer and her conviction that good will win out over evil is paramount to her. "Everything I thought and believed then, I still believe. My opinion hasn't changed. I couldn't dream of changing it,"[25] she says. "I can sing about the problems that occurred under the military. But I also sing about problems that are occurring now. I continue to sing about poverty and hunger, because these are problems that persist under dictatorships and democracies alike."[29]

Although many of the Latin American artists she helps introduce to the public share the same passions, she never allows her ideology to put a limit on who she collaborates with. Quite the contrary—she uses the music to build a bridge between people with different ideologies and is open to working with anybody who wants to work with her. Showing respect toward others is one of her core values. With the confidence she incorporated in her childhood, she rests securely in who she is and can easily embrace diversity without feeling threatened. As she says, "We are all different, and that is the beauty of life on earth. Our different colors, different views, and different political systems."

Her work for peaceful coexistence is rewarded. In October 1996, she receives the CIM-UNESCO Award, granted by the International Music Council, because of her tireless defense of human rights and for her contribution to unity and mutual respect and understanding between people. The jury substantiates its decision by citing her excellent career and the acclaim of her high ethical and moral values.[13]

One year later, in March 1997, she is granted the prestigious position of Vice President of the Earth Council and participates in the drafting of the Earth Charter, which is an ethical framework for building a just, sustainable, and peaceful global society in the twenty-first century.[30]

IN 1987, Mercedes has an exceptional experience at Carnegie Hall.[11] Her performance has come to an end, and she is waiting for the applause to stop, but the audience gets up and continues clapping. She bows with humility and says, "Gracias, mucho gracias." The applause has lasted for three minutes. She expects it to stop soon and spreads her arms out toward the audience as if embracing them while saying, "I love you. Thank you for your love. I love you all. Thank you for coming."

The ovation becomes even more intense. Six minutes have passed. People are still standing. Mercedes is overwhelmed. She never imagined she would be so well-received outside of Latin America. She has never sought popularity or renown. To be here in the United States receiving a standing ovation like this goes beyond her wildest dreams. Mercedes closes her eyes and sucks in the moment, and her life is passing by like a movie on the inside of her eyelids. Here she is, the little girl who always sang, even in the cemetery, receiving tribute—not only because of her voice and her artistic abilities, but because of the life she has lived and the price she has been willing to pay for standing by her beliefs and the pursuit of a better world for everyone.

She feels humble, reflective, and grateful. "Gracias a la vida" has never meant more to her than at this moment. She believes more than ever that what she is fighting for is not in vain.

Mercedes remains standing several minutes more with her eyes still closed before addressing the audience again. With tears running down her cheeks, she says, "Thank you, my beloved friends. I kiss you all. Thank you very much." More than ten minutes have gone by before she leaves the stage, deeply moved. The ovations don't stop until she has left.

DURING THE summer of 1988, Mercedes has a concert tour in West Germany, Switzerland, and Austria together with Joan Baez of the United States, and the German singer Konstantin Wecker. It is an enjoyable time for all three as they have a heartfelt relationship that makes room for much amusement and spontaneity onstage. One of the concerts is released as the DVD, Three Worlds, Three Voices, One Vision.[31] The artists take turns singing, and Mercedes makes an intense impression on Joan Baez:

"Mercedes has built an international reputation by putting her political and social concerns together with her music, combining real artistry with the things she believes in. Short and portly, but with the commanding stage presence of an Andean earth mother and a warm but penetrating alto voice, Ms. Sosa maintains a balance between craft and conviction that endows her music with a searing honesty and power. I have never seen anything like her. She is monumental in stature, a brilliant singer with tremendous charisma who is both a voice and a persona. She may not look like Tina Turner, but she can hold an audience from the stage. When we were singing in concerts together, I would weep all through her set. It embarrassed her, but one night I got down on my knees and kissed her feet. I hadn't been so moved by music in a long time. As far as performers go, she is simply the best."[11]

In October of the same year, Mercedes joins an international music festival in Buenos Aires arranged by Amnesty International, where she performs with such foreign artists as Peter Gabriel and Sting, whom she joins in singing "They Dance Alone." It is about the disappeared in Argentina and a tribute to the Mothers of the Plaza de Mayo, who are present on the stage during the entire concert, which is broadcast on Argentine television.

Bruce Springsteen participates in the festival too. He has just returned from a concert in East Berlin where 300,000 people were gathered, even though only 160,000 tickets had been for sale. Halfway through the concert in Berlin, he had given a speech, saying, "I am not for or against any government. I have come to play rock 'n roll for you, hoping that all walls will one day be demolished." The place had become completely quiet. People had been holding their breath to see how the authorities would react. But when they realized there was nothing the authorities could do because there were too many of them, the crowd had begun cheering without restraint.[32]

It isn't the concert or the speech in itself that brings down the Berlin Wall on November 9, 1989, but together they help give German citizens the courage to go out onto the streets and demand freedom. The example confirms to Mercedes that art can impact the world more than politics. "Culture is the most important revolution. Governments don't last. Culture is the greatest power,"[33] she declares and carries on, using her art and her position as a launchpad to influence the world.

MERCEDES GETS frequent television and talk show invitations. In 1993, she participates in a youth show hosted by the popular Brazilian host, Maria da Graça Xuxa Meneghel, better known just as Xuxa. The studio is full of excited teenagers cheering as Xuxa leads Mercedes into the showroom. It is right before Christmas, so Mercedes starts out with "Ay Navidad" (Oh Christmas), which makes the youngsters clap along tirelessly. Afterward, she hugs the musicians and Xuxa, who obviously is very fond of her and keeps holding and stroking Mercedes' hands. In the background, teenagers cheer, "Olé, Olé, Olé, Olé. Negra, Negra." Mercedes wishes them all a Merry Christmas and is on her way out when Xuxa and the teenagers start to sing "Y dale alegría a mi corazón" (And Give Joy to Your Heart).

The studio sounds like a football stadium, and the temperature rises as the song is repeated over and over again by the sweaty teenagers, who jump and dance with forceful enthusiasm. Mercedes, being close to her sixties, is still able to rock out with the youth. Decisively, she grabs the microphone again and begins to sing along with them. In the middle of the song she notices a little girl with Down syndrome trying to make her way to her. Mercedes stops singing, bows

down and hands her the microphone. The girl sings out bold-
ly while Mercedes strokes her hair. When the girl is finished,
Mercedes looks down at her with tenderness, pride, and acceptance. Then she looks up and smiles at the audience, a
smile that without any words tells everyone they are beautiful in their own way and deserve love and approval.[34]

UP THROUGH the eighties and well into the nineties,
Mercedes is constantly on the move. She gives hundreds of
concerts in Latin America, and she releases a new album almost every year. When she is not travelling, the studio is her
second home. But more essential than the income and the
awards she receives is the love she meets from ordinary people wherever she goes. She has never pursued fame or applause but has been driven by a desire to have a genuine relationship with ordinary citizens. She has worked deliberately
to achieve this by being accessible and paying attention
when someone approaches her. "I've struggled, to reach the
ordinary people, people in the slums, and I could never make
it. It's been a tremendous desperation of mine. It has taken
me many years to attain the love and connectedness with the
people,"[25] she admits. Now she can't step outside her door
without fans approaching in hopes of a greeting. When she
walks around in some of her favorite outdoor markets in
Buenos Aires, her fellow citizens gather around her asking
her to sing. Sometimes she gives in and the crowd sings
along with her. Her fame hasn't corrupted her. Being down-
to-earth, she easily gets into conversation with everyday ad-

mirers. "I am of the people, and I will continue to be of the people." For this reason, she doesn't like to be called a diva. "I hate that word. I am a folk singer,"[25] she maintains.

On one of her few days off, she takes a walk to the old harbor, La Boca, in Buenos Aires. On the way she is approached as usual and, not being in a hurry, takes her time to speak with her admirers. An elderly man comes out from his house and hands her a present—a ceramic bowl with small shards. His shirt is full of holes and some of his teeth are missing. He hugs her and she responds to his warm embrace, thanking him for the present, which probably is the only thing he has to give.[25]

Arriving at the harbor, she sees piles of scrap iron and old shipwrecks that remind her of the seven million immigrants who came to Argentina from Europe in the late nineteenth and early twentieth centuries, people escaping from war and starvation and dreaming of starting a better life. "This part of Buenos Aires has always touched me a lot. It is a very special area. When I see these ships, I think of how far people have travelled and the price they have paid to get here. The hearts of the workers are rusty too, and only peace and democracy can make things better for them," she says in the documentary *Sera Possible el Sur?* (Is it Possible for the South?).

She leaves the harbor and moves further into the heart of La Boca. As she looks around and sees the gaudy, cheerful, multicolored houses in the area around the harbor, she realizes it looks exactly like places she has seen in Italy. And it was in fact mostly Italian immigrants who settled here at La Boca. Unfortunately, most of them also got stuck here. Few of La Boca's residents have gotten the life they were hoping for. Many were farmers who wished to cultivate their own land in a new country, but back then all the land in Argentina also belonged to big estate owners, and there wasn't room for them. As a result, most were stuck in Buenos Aires and forced to get work at the harbor, at the railway, or in industry instead. La Boca is a worker's district, and people here still work hard to make a reasonable living. Reflecting on the Argentine identity and history, Mercedes recalls a saying that is often used to describe the Argentines:

"Mexicans originate from the Aztecs, Peruvians originate from the Incas, and the Argentines originate from the boats."

At a street corner, she bumps into two young men in dirty blue work clothes. In her mind, she makes a connection between the young men with their hands black from oil and the history she has just been thinking of. Her heart goes out to the shy young men, who are obviously overwhelmed by meeting their icon right in the middle of their district and don't know what to do or say. Mercedes stretches her arms out toward them. With both hands around one of the young boy's face, she stands still and holds his gaze for a long time. Her eyes are shining with love, sympathy, and pride. Like a mother who looks at her son with a warm and tender gaze, her expression sends him the most important message a human being can ever receive. A look that says, "I see you. In my eyes you are wonderful." She kisses him on both cheeks before she lets her hands slide down to his shoulders, where they rest appreciatively. Then she turns to the other young man to give him the same attention. With her arm around one of the men's shoulders, they walk together down the street while they keep talking.[25]

Mercedes has developed a unique ability to see and appreciate people for who they are. It makes her happy to get so close to people, but it also makes her tired, bearing other people's burdens, barely getting any time on her own. There are moments where she wishes that she was just an ordinary, anonymous person. "Those who lead a private life have to be happy," she says.

She has gained the closeness with the public she has always hoped for, but it comes at a price.

Mercedes Sosa with Sting

Mercedes doing an interview in her Buenos Aires apartment on May 7, 1999. She often used interviews as an opportunity to speak on behalf of people in Latin America. "The people in Latin America is a suffering people. They are a very poor people. They don't deserve this poverty. We've been robbed of so much, really," she proclaimed regularly

Top left: Mercedes Sosa in an embrace with the Argentine rock star
Charly Garcia, January 27, 1997.

Bottom left: Italian tenor Luciano Pavarotti walks alongside Mercedes Sosa into the ballroom of a local hotel before beginning a press
conference, April 20, 1999. Pavarotti and Sosa sang together for the
first time in a concert in the Boca Juniors soccer stadium, Buenos
Aires, Argentina, April 23, 1999.

Top right: Argentine ex-president Raul Alfonsin in this file photo
taken June 20, 2007. Alfonsin was president from 1983 to 1989 and
won international admiration for putting on trial and jailing the
former military leaders who tortured and killed thousands during the
Dirty War.

Top left: Argentine rock star Charly Garcia and one of the founders of Mothers of the Plaza de Mayo, Hebe de Bonafini, during an open concert in Buenos Aires, February 27, 1999.

Bottom left: Members of the human rights group Grandmothers of the Plaza de Mayo gather outside Argentina's Government House on June 27, 1996 for their one thousandth weekly Thursday march.

Top right: Argentina's President Cristina Fernández de Kirchner holds hands with Estela de Carlotto, president of the human rights organization Grandmothers of the Plaza de Mayo, and Jorge Castro Rubel, who was stolen as an infant. His parents were victims of Argentina's Dirty War, and he had just discovered his true identity.

Top left: During the Rio-plus-five environmental summit in Rio de Janeiro, on March 16, 1997, a journalist asked Mercedes about the situation of the landless, which still hadn't been solved. She commented, "It is absurd, just absurd, that this problem exists. Not just in Brazil, but elsewhere around the hemisphere.

Button left: Mercedes Sosa and Argentina's President Cristina Fernández de Kirchner in 2008, in Buenos Aires.

Top right: Former Argentine dictator Jorge Rafael Videla, is escorted handcuffed by Argentine policemen to a courthouse on the outskirts of Buenos Aires, July 13, 2012. Videla defended the war against his own people by saying, "The oppression is only happening to a minority, who we don't count as Argentines."

Mercedes often took off her long scarf and swung it above her head as she danced onstage. She radiated with well-being and connected with her audience. She was a far more outgoing person when she returned from exile, and her stage presence was enormous.

Mercedes Sosa and Fito Páez during the recording of the double CD, *Cantora*, in 2009.

Mercedes Sosa sings at a concert in the Metropolitan Theater in Mexico City, October 19, 2000

Watercolor by Gustavo Leonel Muñoz Cervio
Proyecto Culturel Mercedes Sosa Por Siempre

Illness and the Last Years

I T IS LATE AT NIGHT. Mercedes is lying alone in the darkness listening to the alarm clock tick while she tosses and turns in bed. She gets up, makes herself a glass of hot milk, drinks it, and goes back to bed. All the impressions from the recording of the new album with Charly García, Alta Fidelidad (High Fidelity), are travelling in her mind like an underground train at rush hour. One thought follows after another. How did the recordings go? Did they make any mistakes? Can they do better in the morning? Her expectations for herself as an artist drain her energy. She wants all her recordings to be perfect, as she knows they will be out in the world forever.[15] They have always been among her greatest challenges; her perfectionism is a breeding ground for worries, but for new ideas as well. She knows that she will make corrections tomorrow, and just thinking about it makes her feel exhausted.

Mercedes' thoughts not only make her worry about the next day; they also extend back into the past. There are so many impressions from the eventful life she has had. Her years in exile and Pocho's death pop with greatest insistence from her inner being. Sometimes when she is surrounded by people she wishes to be alone. Yet when she is alone she misses having people around her. Instinctively, she knows that as long as she can keep herself busy, the dark thoughts will be kept at bay. Her memories are like small gray clouds passing in the sky. As she says, "When I enter a depression the color gray fills my head. I become invaded. The color gray is serious, very serious. It is like a dark cloud is overpowering me. I have to protect myself and escape this color."[3] It is three o'clock in the morning when she finally succeeds to push the gray clouds away and go to sleep. In less than five hours, she has to get up and record again.

She is tired when she wakes, but the gray is gone. However, when night comes, it starts all over again. After the last curtain call, when the lights on the stage are turned off and the door to her flat is locked behind her, the color gray comes sneaking in like a monster ready to devour her.

In 1997, after finishing recording *High Fidelity*, the gray clouds surround Mercedes like a heavy duvet. All her life she has been driven forward by her work and success, and now it is time to pay the bill for not having listened to the accompanying signals from her body and soul. One morning she can't get out of bed and stays there. From all corners of her mind, repressed memories emerge. Her system is overloaded by the good as well as the bad, and the pain stemming from recollecting them both.

The cloudiness that surrounds her turns into a massive depression. The depression causes gastric complications[20] that make her voice shut down, just like when she was in exile.[19] The thought of food sickens her and she stops drinking and eating, notwithstanding Fabián's many attempts to make her do so. For five weeks she consumes only four grapes a day and she loses thirty kilos in five months. She becomes so weak and dehydrated that she needs help to get out of bed to go to the toilet. Sometimes she is groggy and thinks her bedroom is a hotel room. All she wants is to die, and her doctor tells her that she will if she doesn't start taking care of herself.[4]

He gives her injections and prescribes antidepressants. Slowly, she begins to eat, but whatever she eats comes up again. One day she does try to get out of bed, but manages only to make it ten meters before dropping. Later, when she catches a glimpse of herself in the bathroom mirror, she becomes terrified by the look of her worn-out body.

Her doctor and her psychiatrist unanimously diagnose her condition as a severe depression and blame the European exile and years of heavy work. Mercedes agrees with them. "I never thought I had problems. The problems were inside, but deep inside,"[19] she concludes.

Mercedes wants to be left alone, and the only people she sees are Fabián, her doctor, and Maria, a domestic helper, and she only sees them because she has to. Sometimes she gets angry when they come into her bedroom, especially if they bring her food.

After almost a year in solitude, a young singer from Bolivia asks if she can visit Mercedes. Mercedes is very fond of this particular singer and makes an exception. The girl steps into Mercedes' bedroom and is shocked to see Mercedes pale and depleted in her bed. She searches her mind to find the right words. Then she tells Mercedes that she will ask the "Bolivian Mothers" to send a special songbird to sing and cheer her up. The next morning, Mercedes can hear the most beautiful chirping outside her window. She has never heard this bird before and never hears it again after this day.[4]

Mercedes has grown up within the norms of Catholicism and she has always respected the religion of others, but she has never let religion play an active role in her personal life before. Now, in the dark night of her soul, her anger and frustrations are turned toward God, whom she holds responsible for all the injustice she has faced. In doing so, she gets some of her anger and resentment out and she feels something is lifting inside of her. The bitterness turns into gratefulness for life, and instead of wanting to die, she says: "I spent five months in bed unable to walk, thinking I would never do anything again in my life. Now I have so much love for life. I rejoice over life. Life is so great. I have noticed that we often take life for granted. I made peace with God. When you are ill, only you know how much you suffer. The illness has brought me closer to God. I have been reunited with him."[6]

After this experience, Mercedes finally finds the inner strength to get up and return to life with the help and support of her family and friends. The color gray is still around, but she doesn't fear it anymore. She has learned how to deal with it and she is determined not to let it overpower her again.

Looking back after a concert in Miami in 2007, she says emotionally, "I am so grateful, you know, that God gave me this second chance. I never believed in God, but when my illness peaked a few years ago, I was so desperate that I said to him, just like Christ said, 'God, why have you forsaken me?' because I felt abandoned. And it was a miracle, I started to heal."[20]

106

THE DEPRESSION has kept her away from the spotlight for almost a year. She is now sixty-three years old and feels far from energetic. The thought of travelling all over the world makes her consider if it is time to retire, and she doubts that it is possible to make a comeback at her age at all. One part of her wants to settle down and spend more time with her family; another part wants to sing for people as long as she can. She hasn't made up her mind, but life points her in the right direction when she shows herself in public for the first time after her illness at a concert by Pablo Milanés at Luna Park in Buenos Aires. Pablo starts with the song "Años," which he often used to sing with Mercedes. Spontaneously he passes a microphone to her where she is seated in the front row and asks her to sing with him. She does so, for the first time in what feels like ages. She remains calm through it, but her fellow colleagues who know what she has just been through are all crying. A bouquet of flowers is passed to her, and the audience surrounding her stands and begins applauding.[4] It is a moment that gives Mercedes the courage to bounce back.

The first inquiry she accepts after her break is for a concert at Luna Park in 1998. Once again, her fear of not attracting an audience anymore is put to rest. She has long conquered the stage fright and the embarrassment about her weight. Now she moves confidently about onstage as if it is her second home, transforming it into a cozy living room with a big chair for her to sit in the middle of the stage. The audience is invited to be her personal guests. She gives them her undivided attention in a relaxed and humorous way. She laughs a lot and makes her audience laugh along with her. Speaking with a tender voice, she enters what seems like a personal dialogue with thousands of people when she chats spontaneously between her songs. A giant screen above the stage gives the audience the advantage of contemplating her gestures and expressions down to the last detail.

She surprises herself and her audience by the energy she has throughout her performance. A journalist asks her afterward where she gets all her energy from. She replies, "I have no clue. I felt very, very weak."[35] After a while, she notices that something good happens to her while she sings and concludes that she is actually healing herself by doing so.

She also starts recording again. Her first recording after her illness is Misa Criolla, a spiritual musical composition, for which she is invited to participate in by the Argentine composer Ariel Ramírez. Mercedes sees it as a sign from above that the recording takes place right after she made peace with God. Likewise, she thinks it is no coincidence that the album is being recorded in Israel.[6] She hasn't become religious in the traditional sense and doesn't feel she needs to change the way she lives, but her newfound spirituality has made her aware of a divine presence within. Even if she has never been preoccupied with religion, she hasn't sung or spoken up against God either. She has always respected others' religion, especially her mother's.[36] Throughout life, Ema has been an example to Mercedes when it comes to converting religion into practice by being charitable. To love your neighbor as you love yourself is the overall guideline to Mercedes as well. Otherwise, she doesn't speak a lot about her faith or how she pictures God. She doesn't have to. Her deeds speak louder than words, and from her way of being in this world, she is deeply tied to love—perhaps so deeply that love is her God.

MERCEDES HAS always been close to her mother. Her closeness is such that alone at a friend's house one night, she suddenly feels that someone is standing behind her, placing a hand on her shoulder in the same way her mother used to do. Mercedes turns around, but no one is there. A few minutes later, she receives a phone call that her mother has fallen unconscious. Even if it isn't a shock—her mother has been sick for a long time—it affects Mercedes deeply. On April 27, 2000, her mother dies at eighty-nine.[4]

For every time Mercedes loses someone she loves she feels the grief gets worse. But this time she knows she needs to face it head-on instead of running away from it. She tries to find the balance and allow herself the time to grieve without letting the color gray invade her. She finds comfort and strength in her last recording, *Misa Criolla*, which pays tribute to her mother's strong faith in God. She receives her first Grammy, for *Misa Criolla*, the Latin Grammy Award for Best Folk Album.

DESPITE BEING physically weakened by the adversity of life and the effect of age sneaking up on her, Mercedes manages to move on with her career. But she notices that something has changed. "After the depression in 1997 and the death of my mother in 2000, I feel doomed to some kind of constant sensitivity," she says. She cries more easily when she is alone, and in front of people as well. Sometimes she feels overwhelmed by gratefulness for being alive, being able to sing for people and over receiving so much love in return. "I sing for people because I love them,"[25] she says, and adds that it is the love of people that gives her strength.

Other people's struggles move her deeply too. After her shows, she takes her time to relate with them and listen to their stories, as she did after a concert in Holland. "When I met Mercedes Sosa, a good friend of mine was her tour manager. I feel privileged to have met her and remember how impressed I was with her grace and humbleness when she met with a long line of admirers after having sung a full-length concert. If she was tired, nobody noticed. She was completely focused on every story that was shared with her that night. Impressive!" Christel Veraart, composer-singer, Alaska.[37]

One night after a concert at a public festival in Tunyan, 140 km south of Mendoza, Mercedes' basist Genoni tells her that he has met one of her fans in the reception of the Grand Hotel. The fan, Luis Plaza Ibarra, has come all the way from Sweden for the sole purpose to experience Mercedes live, but he can't find any accommodation as all the hotels in the area are fully booked. When Mercedes hears this she sends a lady to invite Luis to meet her backstage after the concert. The security controls will let him through without any trouble if he just tells them that Mercedes has invited him. Backstage he first meets Fabián, who says that his mother is very weak and he is not sure if she can manage to see him. Nevertheless, despite feeling weak, Mercedes shows up. Standing eye to eye with her so suddenly, Luis' mind goes blank and he just grabs her hand and says, "Thank you, thank you for everything," to which Mercedes responds, "Have you found a place to sleep tonight?" This meeting begins a friendship that never stops, and Luis ends up touring with Mercedes the last eight years of her life.

For every crisis Mercedes goes through she becomes additionally compassionate and understanding. She can identify with the poor, the sick, the divorced, with women who have had an abortion, with people who have lost their loved ones, with the lonely, the depressed, and the suicidal. Her personal afflictions enable her to be empathic and to pass on comfort, as an American journalist watched her do toward Juan Carlos Nagel, a colleague, backstage after a concert. "I watched her once cradle an Argentine journalist backstage at a UCLA concert. She'd known him in the 1970s in Argentina before he moved to L.A. He was dying of AIDS, and they both knew it would be the last time they'd see one another. He lost his public composure, fell into her arms crying, 'Mama!' She held him tenderly. The rest of us left the room holding back tears. Once again I was reminded of her beauty, her humanity. She was a true *pacha mama*, Incan word for a powerful woman, an earth mother."[38] Tom Schnabel, radio producer, *Rhythm Planet*.

Various people come just to be in the healing atmosphere that seems to take shape during her concerts. It is not unusual that some people cry all the way through. Even if they don't speak or understand a word of Spanish, the message is understood by the way Mercedes performs. Without any sound, the story will still be told by her use of facial expressions and body language alone. Mercedes' language is heart language; it doesn't need any interpretation. Her body, her expressions, her intonation are all in complete accordance with the emotion she is expressing. Her face is constantly alive, and her distinctive black eyebrows bring out the intensity in her exotic black eyes. When she smiles, it discharges into two soft dimples, and the sound of her smile can be heard in her voice.

"Her face is as unforgettable as the voice, matching its chords in power and presence."[39] Sandra Bertrand, Galo Magazine.

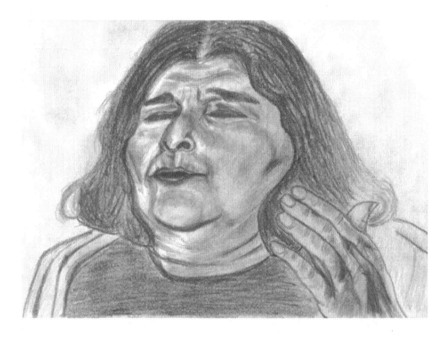

Her enormous impact on all kinds of people is evident when she returns to the northern part of Argentina after her personal crisis. In March 2001, she gives a long outdoor concert in Santa Catalina, a mining town 3,770 meters above sea level. The stage has been set up on a small island in a swirling river that keeps it separate from the audience, mainly poor miners who have showed up in spite of the cold weather. In the middle of the performance, all of a sudden a troubled young man in ragged clothes jumps into the river and swims his way to Mercedes onstage. He takes off his T-shirt and passes it to her. Standing with his upper body naked, he gives her an affectionate squeeze, to which she responds while she keeps on singing.[40] What is running through the young man's mind? Is he drugged, or is he simply one of the many who has a need to be seen and accepted for who he is? Has Mercedes become a mother figure to him in his imagination, in the same way she has for many of her fans? One who felt this was Ian Malinow, a Latin music correspondent and blogger from Costa Rica, who said, "In a way, Sosa was to me like one more family member. More than a singer, in a twisted, surrealistic world of mine, she became like an imaginary, globe-trotting grandmother to me. Don't ask me why, but she seemed to have that inherent power over her faithful listeners and admirers."[41]

It doesn't embarrass Mercedes that some of her fans relate to her as a mother figure. She even validates their strong feelings about her. One night a young man, Ignacio, walks with the crowd to the back entrance of the theatre hoping to greet Mercedes after a show. "There was a turmoil and the guards announced that Mercedes had already left the building. I could see that Fabián was still around talking on his mobile, so I assumed Mercedes was around too. I felt nervous and anxious as I waited next to the elevator. After a few minutes I saw her through the glass door. When the door opened I reached out my left hand and Mercedes grabbed it. Holding her little hand in mine I walked her to the car. She got into the backseat and somehow I managed to ask Fabían if I could talk to her. Then the amazing thing happened. Mercedes signaled to me that I should come and sit next to her. I couldn't believe it. I got into the backseat but I didn't know what to do or what to say. So many thoughts went through my head. All I could say was: 'Mercedes, can I give you a kiss?' She looked at me, smiled, and said, 'But son, why should you not give me a kiss?' I kissed her on her right cheek. I remember her very rich perfume. Then I got off the car, the doors closed, Mercedes left, and I wasn't the same anymore."

Mercedes is aware of the influence she has on people and wonders whether it is her voice, her face, or her belief that makes the deep impact.[4] "I'm not young or beautiful, but I've got my voice and the soul that comes out in my voice," she concludes in an interview in 2001.[42] When she sings, everything inside her comes out, and the audience gets a glimpse of her soul. But it is not only the soft, emotional expressions she masters. She can also be dramatic and commanding. She possesses a natural authority, which she manages to channel by raising her arms, clenching her fists, or throwing her head back in laughter. One of her most fiery performances is the song "Cuando Tengo la Tierra," which once got her arrested. When she sings it, she walks fast back and forth on the stage. Between the verses she raises her volume in a proclamation that shows the strength of her voice. It can start a revolution on the spot without the use of any microphones. Once, a sound system broke down when she started singing. "I remember Mercedes Sosa for her interpretation of "Los Mareados" at the Concertgebouw in Amsterdam, where I attended a concert by her. For this song, Mercedes decided to open standing with her back to the audience. Her first notes must have taken the sound engineer by surprise, because the speakers all of a sudden blew out with a terrible noise." Christel Veraart, composer-singer, Alaska.[38]

In 2002, after the recording of *Acústico en Vivo*, a live recording for which she wins her second Grammy, she becomes ill again–this time physically. She has to cancel all her scheduled concerts, and her illness keeps her away from performing for two years, although she manages to support the election of Néstor Kirchner in 2003.

Soon after taking office in May, Kirchner dismisses powerful military and police officials. Stressing the need to increase accountability and transparency in government, Kirchner overturns the amnesty laws for military officers accused of torture and assassinations during the Dirty War. By nullifying the amnesty laws, the case against Videla, together with fourteen other generals responsible for the Dirty War, is reopened. They are charged with murder, torture, and kidnappings and sentenced to life in prison. This time the judge makes sure that amnesty is not possible and they cannot escape the consequences of their acts. Mercedes is relieved that justice seems to finally prevail in her country.

Videla is sent to an ordinary prison where he dies from a fall in the shower on May 17, 2013. During his court case, he still defended his barbarian acts against humanity. A new arrest warrant is issued on Isabel Perón, but it hasn't been possible to arrest her because she has escaped to Spain, and the Spanish government refuses to extradite her to Argentina.

When Mercedes returns after her hiatus in 2005, she suffers from chronic back pain from some serious falls that almost paralyzed her. It stops her from dancing as she used to, but even with tremendous back pain, she finds a way to deliver what people expect, and her concerts remain sold-out. Her first performance after her return in 2005 is in the Argentine Congress in Música en el Salón Blanco (Music in the White Hall) and has a TV audience of one million viewers. She is paid tribute by the first lady, Cristina Fernández Kirchner, ministers, government officers, and several other Argentine artists. Together with guests León Gieco and Teresa Parodi, she sings many of the classic folk songs that have made her famous. She also sings songs from her new CD, Corazón libre, which is released in 2005 and earns Mercedes her third Grammy.

IN February 2007, Mercedes goes to Mendoza for a holiday. She is thrilled to be back at the place where she once fell in love and the Manifesto of the New Song Movement, which has influenced her life ever since, was drafted. She is now in her early seventies, and she wants time to reflect on her life in peaceful, quiet surroundings far from the chaotic jumble of Buenos Aires.

Standing by the window, she faces her big garden with the majestic old trees. As she looks out, she sees a reflection of herself in the glass. She studies the landscape of wrinkles on the map of her face. They all tell a story—her story. A story about a woman who was fortunate to grow up in a loving and supporting family, who possessed an obvious talent, and always did what she enjoyed the most. A woman who never dreamt of getting such an exciting life, travelling all over the world, and receiving so much recognition. She never strived after any of this. Life must have handpicked her, she thinks, as the scenery on her face turns into a smile. On her forehead, she also observes the deep canyons formed by tragic events. Unwelcome changes have pushed her in directions she didn't want to go. However, in the end, they have led her to her destination as she held on to the hand of acceptance, the only guide knowing the path through the wilderness of change. "Todo cambia" runs like a red thread through her life, making it a constant journey. "I have had a very beautiful and a very tragic life,"[3] she says out loud and turns away from the window. She has to prepare for an interview, or so she thinks.

In another part of the country, a group of sixty enthusiastic, young singers gets on a bus headed for Mendoza.

The only thing on Mercedes' schedule during her stay in Mendoza is an appointment with the Argentine reggae singer and composer Bahiano, who has been granted an interview for a documentary about folklore in Latin America for the program MP3.[43] It is about to start, and she is sitting in the two-seat Chesterfield sofa wearing a pink dress with white embroidery while waiting expectantly for the cameraman to get ready. He explains that in order to get the best shots, the curtains toward the street need to be pulled. She has no idea that it is all a part of a set-up and that she is in for a wonderful surprise.

The interview starts. Mercedes feels relaxed, in a good mood. They have already spent ten minutes looking at old photos, and she has told the reporter how important her family is to her. She has even sung one of her favorite songs for him. The cameraman has let the windows to the street remain open, and the curtains are moving a little. Bahiano asks Mercedes if she likes serenades and she confirms. Suddenly, Mercedes hears singing coming from the street. She looks stunned at the journalist, who gets up from his chair and reaches out for her hand while helping her carefully stand up. Slowly they move toward the window, and he pulls the curtains aside. In complete amazement, she sees a crowd of young people who are singing polyphonic "Tonada de la viejo amor" (Tune of Old Love). It sounds fabulous. Mercedes gazes with admiration, and it doesn't take her long to join in.

When finished, she wipes tears from her eyes, shouts, "Bravo, bravo, bravo," thanks them and asks for another. The group then starts singing "Luna tucumana" (Tucumán's Moon). Afterward Bahiano leads a walking-impaired but extremely cheerful Mercedes out to the street, where she is serenaded with "Zamba por vos" (Zamba for You).[44] It is a celebration none of them will ever forget.

MERCEDES REMAINS politically active, and in 2007 she supports the election of Cristina Fernández de Kirchner, wife of Nestór Kirchner, who wins and becomes Argentina's first elected female president. Mercedes accepts an invitation to sing at the inauguration celebration in front of the Government Palace on December 10. The Kirchner administration's policies are having tremendous impact for the working class, whose exploitation Sosa so fervently has denounced in many of her songs.

Despite her poor health, Mercedes continues to travel all over the world. She suffers from respiratory problems; her voice is not as strong, but it remains an admirable instrument. It is rich and dynamic but also malleable and stunningly expressive. Her vibrato has grown wider with age, but she uses it with restraint. She is determined to continue singing for as long as she can.

2008 is a very active year for her. On May 18, Mercedes performs together with the popular Colombian singer Shakira, in Buenos Aires. They sing the song "La maza" at a huge outdoor aid concert for marginalized Latin American children. She also travels to Europe and Israel and gives several concerts at Carnegie Hall, in New York. Due to severe back pain, she is now bound to sit in a wheelchair onstage, but it doesn't stop her from standing up for a moment to take a few of her characteristic zamba dance steps each time. When she does, the audience is cheering.

Having completed the tour, Mercedes starts planning the recording of another CD, *Cantora*. She has spoken with the record company about it already. She envisions it as a double CD consisting of a number of songs she has never recorded before, and with guest contributors she has a special affection for. The producer at Sony thinks it is a great idea and supports her choosing both songs and artists. She sends out personal invitations and receives acceptances across the board. It is an honor for them to be part of the project, they say. It is also an opportunity for Mercedes to reunite with friends she hasn't seen for a long time. The Brazilian singer Caetano Veloso, for instance. When laying eyes on him again in the studio, she finds herself forced to dry her eyes with a handkerchief. "Darling, how are you? My dear brother, it's been so long since we last saw each other. I love you so much, Caetano. I have tears of joy for you,"[3] she says.

Charly García, the rock singer, sings a beautiful and emotional song, "Desarma y sangra" (Disarms and Bleeds), about being in the school of life. The lyrics assert that there isn't any school that can teach you how you have to live. Charly has been through a difficult time prior to the recordings, and Mercedes, who has been worried about him, says to him, "I feel a weird happiness within me. I have never seen you like this before. What a beautiful song. How pretty, my beautiful prince."[3] Then they begin to dance in the middle of the floor of the studio while everyone else stands in a circle around them clapping. After their little dance, they retreat to a brown leather sofa where Charly puts his arm around her and she rests, content in his arms.

The recordings take place in a free and easy atmosphere marked by honesty, humor, and mutual respect. Mercedes' voice is still strong, but it gets tired more easily, so she studies each song at length before recording it. She wants it to be perfect on the first or second try to save her voice. Her memory is impeccable. Mercedes knows all her songs by heart, and keeps the text in front of her just as a formality. At seventy-three, she still has high expectations for herself: "This will be heard all over the world forever, and if we don't get it right, we will hate ourselves forever for not having sung the song the right way."[4] When they get to the recording of "Zamba del cielo" (Zamba of Heaven), with Fito Páez and Liliana Herrero, the whole studio trembles as if heaven touches earth. Afterward there is complete silence, and they take each other's hands. Liliana breaks out in tears and Mercedes cries, "Oh my God. It is insane. I had goose bumps all the way through the song." The song expresses the feeling Mercedes has when she looks back on her life:

"Life has given me so much. But it has also taken away. Life is like a river of wonders and pain."

In an interview regarding the recording of *Cantora*, Mercedes is asked why it is being recorded at this stage of her career. She answers with a line from the song "Cuchillos" (Knives), by Charly García: "Because I am not going to die."

The last song Mercedes records for *Cantora* is a duet with Pedro Guerra, who is from the Canary Islands. The song is a bonus track for the Spanish edition. It is written by Pablo Milanés to Mercedes especially, and is called **"La soledad"** (Loneliness). She is too weak to get out of her house, so the recording takes place in a small studio that has been set up in a room adjacent to her living room. The song puts words to the loneliness she has experienced throughout her life, but there is no trace of pain in her voice. On the contrary, the last song she sends out into the world is a soothing sound of lapping waves erasing the footprints of loneliness from the shore of the human heart.

Cantora becomes a top seller in Argentina in 2009 and receives the Latin Grammy Award for Best Folk Album.

Top left: Mercedes Sosa with her mother, Ema del Carmen Gíron, in her hometown of Tucumán.

Bottom left: Mercedes Sosa during the wake for her mother, Ema Gíron, April 27, 2000.

Top right: Since early childhood, Mercedes had been reflective, observant, and alert, but after her depression in 1997, she processed sensory data much more deeply, which enabled her to express emotional nuances with more power and precision.

Top left: Mercedes Sosa performs during a concert celebrating the tenth anniversary of the Peres Center for Peace, in Tel Aviv, October 27, 2008.

Bottom left: Colombian pop singer Shakira and Mercedes Sosa perform during "The Concert For The Children," in Buenos Aires, May 17, 2008.

Top right: Argentina's President Cristina Fernández de Kirchner and her husband, outgoing President Néstor Kirchner, stand onstage as Mercedes Sosa sings to celebrate Fernández's inauguration, December 10, 2007.

Mercedes Sosa accepts the award for Best Folk Album, for Misa Criolla, at the Innagural Latin Grammy Awards, September 13, 2000, in Los Angeles.

Buenos Aires, September 18, 2009

SINCE MERCEDES finished the recording of *Cantora* in June, her health has continued downhill. She is standing in her flat looking out at Buenos Aires through the window, framed by the green ferns on her balcony. Fabián will be coming soon to take her to Clinic Trinidad, one of the best hospitals in the Palermo neighborhood of Buenos Aires. She has packed a small bag to bring with her. Her eyes wander around her living room, from the vases abounding with colorful flowers to the long rows of books on her bookshelves and further on to the art she has collected over the years—paintings, sculptures, exotic hand woven carpets covering the floor, and all kinds of indigenous crafts. A portrait decorates the wall in the entry area. It is a drawing made by her cherished old friend Joan Baez. Her eyes stop by all the prizes hanging on the walls. They whisper to her, *We are the proof that your life hasn't been a mistake.* Some prizes mean more to her than others—the prizes she has received in her later years. The Diamond Konex Award, from 1994, for being the most important personality in popular music in Argentina, and two precious prizes from 1996, the Simões Lopes Neto medal, for her artistic and personal merits toward promoting the unity of the people, and the CIM-UNESCO award, are special to her. They are the proof that she has lived to her full potential and fulfilled her destiny. At the end of the day, this means more to her than being recognized worldwide in 1996 as having one of the most remarkable voices in the world.

She responds with a sigh of relief. When Fabián arrives, she continues the conversation with him: "Everything you see here are not just awards for singing. They are also rewards for what I think. I think about human beings. I think about injustice. Maybe if I hadn't thought, my fate would have been different. I would just have been a regular singer. So this is what makes me think I'm not mistaken when I started to have an ideology."[3]

With this conviction, she leaves her home for what turns out to be the last time. During the next three weeks, Mercedes' health worsens. Her kidneys fail, and she has liver and heart problems too. It is complicated by cardio-respiratory problems, and she is put in the intensive care unit.[45] She knows that her situation can turn out to be fatal and allows many of her good friends to come and visit and say goodbye in case she doesn't survive, although she still hopes for a miracle. She loves life, but she doesn't desire to get as old as her mother either. "I would rather move on while I still think clearly," she says.

On Friday evening she asks for her priest, Father Luis Farinello, to come and give her the last oil,[46] a Catholic ritual providing forgiveness of sins as a preparation for a dying person to pass over to eternal life. Father Farinello, who has known Mercedes for years, recounts that conducting the ritual was a very emotional moment for both of them, as Mercedes was conscious and knew she was dying.

The nation is holding its breath when Fabián, outside the hospital, reports on his mother's condition to the news reporters. On Saturday, he says, "We are many who pray for her and believe in a miracle, but her life is in God's hands." Her nephew, Coqui Sosa, confirms, and tells them that Mercedes' official website has collapsed from the vast number of messages of support pouring in during the past few days.[47] "It shows that love gets things moving," he says.

Mercedes wants more than anything to sing for everyone around her until she takes her last breath. But her lungs give out. She is put in a medically induced coma and given artificial respiration while under constant observation. On October 4, at 5:15 a.m., she dies peacefully in her sleep. One of the best voices the world has ever heard has become silent. One of the most loving and passionate hearts has stopped beating.

"She died in peace in her hospital bed as a free woman who had accomplished everything she wanted in life. She lived her seventy-four years to the fullest. She didn't have any type of barrier or any type of fear that limited her,"[47] Fabián proclaims as he meets with the press to announce his mother's death.

Buenos Aires, October 5, 2009

HUNDREDS OF people are gathered on the green lane outside the crematorium at Chacarita Cemetery in Buenos Aires. They clap and sing as white smoke rises straight and quiet from the chimney toward the blue spring sky like an offering of thanks. Like a song without words. Singing for the last time: "GRACIAS A LA VIDA."

"Thanks to life, which has given me so much.
It gave me laughter and it gave me longing.
With them I distinguish happiness and pain.
The two materials from which my songs are formed."
"Gracias a la vida," by Violeta Parra

Mercedes' last wish was that her ashes be spread out in three of her favorite places: "When I die, I wish to be a little bit in Tucumán, a little bit in Mendoza, and a little bit in Buenos Aires." Fabián, along with her two grandchildren, her two brothers, and her nephews, fulfill it. It is one more example of how, in life as well as in death, she always wanted to be everywhere, embracing everybody.

Button right: Fernando and Orlando Sosa, brothers of Mercedes Sosa, and her nephew, Coqui, hold an urn containing her ashes, at Mount San Javier in Tucumán province, October 13, 2009.

Part Two

My Encounter with Mercedes Sosa

"When our lives become pageants, we become actors. When we become actors, we sacrifice authenticity. Without authenticity, we can't cultivate love and connection. Without love and connection, we have nothing."
Brené Brown

HOPEFULLY, PART ONE has given you a good sense of Mercedes Sosa as a person, the events that shaped her, and the impact she had on various people wherever she went. Before we move on to my personal journey with Mercedes, I want to give you a recent example of how she still touches people today.

In the summer of 2015, on my way from Turkey to one of the Greek Islands, I met two wonderful American ladies in a ferry office. They asked about my life and I said I was writing a book about Mercedes Sosa. One of the ladies got so excited that she jumped and hugged me for a long time, before saying, "Are you really writing a book about Mercedes Sosa? She is out of this world. I love her, she is the best. I hardly know anything about her personal life. I really want to read your book." The other lady hadn't heard about Mercedes before, so I started telling her about her life and the influence she had had on me. As I talked, tears began to run down her face. Then she said, "What an amazing story. I want to get to know her too. Your personal story is touching me deeply. This is something others can benefit from hearing too. I am the director of member experiences in a social club for very influential people in New York. I want them to hear this. Maybe you can come and speak when the book gets out?"

The Turkish man working in the office had overheard our conversation and put on "Gracias a la vida" on his iPhone. As the song played, both women commented on the strong presence that filled the office like electricity.

Our Common Humanity

WHEN I FIRST LAID eyes on Mercedes Sosa, she immediately stirred something deep inside of me. I felt a need to connect with her and a desire to get to know her. I embarked on a journey that turned my life around.

As I watched Mercedes on the internet and listened to her voice, whether she was singing or speaking, I felt a connection with her that led to solace. Later I learned that what I was intuitively inspired to do in my recovery from childhood trauma had a positive effect that could be explained scientifically. I realized that the answers could be found in neuroscience—interpersonal neurobiology, in particular.

Interpersonal neurobiology is about how our minds affect one another when we connect with each other. At its core, interpersonal neurobiology believes that we are who we are because of our relationships and that all relationships, especially the most intimate ones, change the brain. It is a generally held belief in neuroscience that the adult brain will continue to grow new brain cells throughout its entire life and remain open to changes in response to experience. The brain never stops developing, and intimate and healthy relationships can continue to influence us throughout life; they are in fact essential in our development because they give us new experiences that strengthen new neural connections and shape the structure of our brain. To know that we can actively influence our brain at any time in our lives and thereby change our lives brings about hope to all of us.

As you read on, you will see how Mercedes Sosa helped me get through one of my biggest life crises by enabling me to heal my existential wounds. Mercedes Sosa became my new focus point, and, in the process, I discovered how the brain responds to music, to mindfulness, to imagination, as well as to positive, personal encounters with others. I believe my story as well as the scientific insights that back up my experience can be useful to anyone who finds him or herself stuck in limiting, crippling, or tormenting experiences from the past. But before I dive into my own journey, let me explain what I mean by 'existential wound.'

An existential wound is a wound many of us get early in life. It can become defining for how we view ourselves for the rest of our lives because it influences our self-worth if we neglect to deal with it properly. Whether we are aware of it or not, most of us carry existential wounds that can be reopened. If you wonder whether you have been wounded existentially, you can take a look at your life and see if there is a theme your life constantly revolves around. If you find yourself repeating a behavior pattern that leads to painful experiences, it is likely that the trigger is an existential wound. Many of us find ways of covering these up, and we limp forward, pretending that they don't exist. Some people are conscious of this, but for many the wound is beyond self-awareness. When life's circumstances conspire to reopen these wounds, we can either run away or see these moments as opportunities to heal and to grow. When we are aware of our existential wounds and what reinjures them, when we know how to handle ourselves with love and care, we don't have to fear them or cover them up. It sets us free to live full, conscious, and authentic lives.

Basic beliefs about our self-image and esteem originate in the formative years of our lives, particularly through interactions with parents. When we are children, the parents—especially the mother—become mirrors for us to see ourselves. We understand our worth through what is reflected back in the eyes of our parents or caretaker. If they look at us with acceptance and love, we will have a self-perception of at least moderate value. Mercedes was very well aware of this. Thanks to the love she received from her parents, she grew into being a healthy adult with a solid foundation of self-worth, which enabled her to follow her heart for her entire life and bounce back whenever she faced trouble later. "I can thank my parents for the peace I experience in my life. Without peace, I wouldn't be able to sing for you. If you have peace in your life, it is because you brought it with you from your childhood. Without their love I would never have become the person I became,"[25] she said.

No matter how good our childhood has been or how good our parents' intentions are, many of us get hurt during our upbringing, whether we are conscious of it or not. It happens because the world isn't perfect. As small children we are sensitive, and the brain has not developed enough to make sense of what is happening. Everything we experience as infants is stored in subconscious memory and shapes our developing personality. One of the first things we learn from the first responses from our caretakers is that we are okay when we achieve something. In order to be *someone*, we must do *something*. When a little child is having a good time on the playground, he will call out in excitement for his caretakers, saying, "Look at me, look at me." What the little child is asking for is the loving attention and confirmation that he is being seen having fun and that he is okay. The automatic response most parents will give in a situation like this is to say, "Yes, you are very good at swinging." Without being aware of it, the adult is leaving a subconscious message in the child that in order to be okay, he must be good, clever, and smart at doing something.

Because of the various value systems that are passed on to us and the narratives that dominate the way society functions, it is very difficult for us to make the shift from living a doing-based life to living a being-based life. As we grow up, we often fail to question the value system that has been passed on to us by the traditions and unwritten rules of the family or culture we grow up in. So we just keep striving to achieve something in order to get approval. When our self-worth equals the success we can measure, we become trapped into leading goal-oriented lives in which we exhaust ourselves.

Imagine how different life could turn out if the response to the child on the playground had been, "Yes, I see you, darling. I love to watch you when you are having such fun. I see how wonderful you are, and you make me very happy." Such a response would lead us to live a life whereby our motivation and energy comes from being who we are and doing what comes naturally to us, just like singing was as natural as walking and talking to Mercedes. Whether we get approval from the outside becomes less relevant when we are at peace with ourselves. Mercedes never planned to get approval or to be rewarded. "When I sing, I sing because I love to sing. Not because I think I will be rewarded,"[3] she said.

When we don't depend on approval from others, we can allow ourselves to be human and be compassionate with ourselves when we make mistakes. Mercedes was a perfectionist with high professional ambitions for herself as an artist, and critics all over the world described her performances as impeccable, but she was realistic and knew that mistakes were unavoidable. "Of course I cannot always give my best in every song," she once admitted.

In all the live performances I have watched, I only noticed Mercedes make one single mistake: the classic mistake of starting ahead of the other musicians. Her reaction to her stumble was amazing. Standing in front of thousands of people, she didn't show any sign of panic or embarrassment. She just smiled peacefully and nodded her head in a gentle way, as if she accepted what she had done and was confirming that she was still okay. Instead of being knocked over, she just carried on with a light laughter in her voice and a smile on her lips. Even if she had high expectations of herself and always wanted to do her best, she didn't allow artistic perfectionism or failure to affect her self-worth. She showed compassion toward herself instead of blaming herself.

Watching this made me understand the connection between our upbringing and the conclusions we make about ourselves when we fail or can't live up to our standards. When we stumble, we can either get back on our feet, shake the dust off, and show compassion toward ourselves, or we can conclude that something is wrong with us. As we saw in part one, Mercedes went through severe struggles, but she always made a comeback, and her self-worth was usually untouched. When I made my first big stumble, I went with the last conclusion and suffered under the burden of my hard judgment for many years.

My Life before Mercedes Sosa

I GREW UP in a small town on the west coast of Denmark in an average family, the oldest child of three. My brother was six years younger than me, and my sister ten years younger. I was a quiet and sensitive kid who picked up on moods easily and sensed if my parents weren't cheerful. In my young mind, the things I picked up on grew quite big. I kept it all to myself because I didn't want to burden my parents. I understood they had their own problems—problems that were not meant to be talked about. One was that my mother suffered from insomnia and that it affected her physically and emotionally. She had fallen and hurt her head badly many times as a child, sustaining seven concussions and two skull fractures. In hindsight, I think that my mum might have had brain damage that affected both her ability to sleep and her ability to show empathy. But such a diagnosis was not available at that time, so all I knew was that there was something wrong with my mum and we had to hide it from the people around us. It was not a part of either our family culture or the Danish culture generally in the '70s to speak openly about personal problems. The fear of what other people might think made my mother's problem the family secret. Not out of ill will, but more out of lack of understanding, my mum confided in me about the secret and wanted me to keep it. The well-being of my mother meant the well-being of our family, so the first thing I would think about when I got up in the morning was whether my mother had slept or not. If she hadn't, we would often have to cancel our plans for the day, and the atmosphere in the house would become dark and oppressive.

My dad was a good man who worked hard to provide for his family. He never hurt my siblings or me, but he was evasive and passive when it came to raising us and left it to my mother. He supported my mother practically, but he didn't show affection easily and wasn't able to give his children much emotional support either.

At ten, my mother began sharing deeply personal things with me. Often she would cry and ask for advice. I was so understanding, she said. Sometimes when my mum was overwhelmed by fatigue she would get upset and lock herself in the bedroom. I was afraid of what she was doing in there and tried to make her open the door. If I heard her cry I became tense and went into my room with a knot in my stomach. Sometimes I stuffed my mouth with a pillow so no one would hear me cry because I knew I had to be strong. I would come out afterward with a smile and tell jokes to make everyone laugh, suppressing how I felt. I became a master in suppressing my real feelings, and, like Mercedes, I would face the consequences of doing so many years later.

I also helped out with cooking, cleaning, and looking after my siblings. I was aware that I had an important role in the family as my mother's little helper, friend, stand-in emotional husband, and adviser. I was told how special I was when I supported her, and I understood that I was valuable because of all the things I did in order to keep our family together.

My mother's condition affected me psychologically. I developed an oversensitivity to her suffering, which made me worry about her constantly and dread that she would die—she often told me that she didn't expect to live long. I felt guilty when I was not with her, and I didn't allow myself to be cheerful if she was in the dumps. When my friends were partying, I would be on my knees praying, asking God to heal her and bring peace to our family. I felt my mother was living her life inside of me to such a degree that I didn't live my own life.

Almost like Mercedes, but for different reasons, I went into 'self-imposed exile' to get away from the pain and left home at the age of fifteen, with my parents' blessings. I moved in with a loving and caring couple who didn't have children of their own. They treated me as their own and poured immense love and affection onto me, and for the first time I could unleash my anxiety and pain. Their support was priceless during my adolescence, but it would take thirty more years for me to get free from the fear, guilt, and oversensitivity that ruled my life because I didn't have insight into the extent of my wounds yet.

My parents both did the best they could. Looking back, I am grateful for the values they passed on to me. But before I could reach this point, I had to go through the long process of grappling with how my childhood affected the way I was living my life as an adult.

LOOKING ON the bright side of it all, my entrusted role in our family made me autonomous and adventurous. I had learned to take initiative and be inventive, and I had a feeling that I could do whatever I wanted in life. So right after high school I set out into the world, bolstered with self-confidence, but lacking in self-worth. I trusted my abilities to achieve well but didn't rest secure in my innermost being, like Mercedes did. She achieved because of who she already was, while I tried to become someone by achieving. Travelling was probably a way to get as far away from the pain as possible, but the psychological umbilical cord to my mother was so tenacious that even when I went to the far end of the earth I could sense whether my mother was happy or not.

I had grown up to become a caring, responsible adult and a good problem solver who made an effort to make sure people around me were content. As a result, people spoke well of me and trusted me. Being a hard worker who gladly worked her bum off and never thought about her own needs or gave herself much rest, I harvested the recognition that made me feel important. What I wasn't aware of was that I was using the same survival strategy that helped me feel unique in my childhood. Taking responsibility for others was the strategy I had subconsciously developed in order to survive as a child. As an adult, I thought that this was just the way I was as a person. I didn't know it was something I might be able to adjust, nor that if I didn't, it could drive me toward a massive collapse.

I began to feel exhausted at a very young age. Even after a holiday, I didn't feel refreshed; it was as if my batteries didn't charge. I tried to hide it because I was embarrassed about being so tired, and I didn't want to wallow in self-pity or be a burden to anyone. I had learned that being tired was something that had to be hidden or covered up, so, even when I was exhausted, I kept pushing myself onward. People came to me with their problems and I was always available. Saying no wasn't an option because I genuinely cared about people and I wasn't aware that I was subconsciously motivated by my need to be indispensable.

IN 1988 I was bringing a team of seven people to India to assist an Indian couple in developing a Christian charity organization with a vision to establish children homes and educate people in the slums of Mumbai. I was only twenty-three and busy trying to "save the world" when I realized that one of the team members had criticized me and questioned my integrity behind my back. We had just spent six weeks in Mumbai, where four of us girls had shared a bedroom with only two beds. I had been sleeping on an air mattress on the floor next to another girl. After backbreaking work in the humid, smelly, chaotic, and overcrowded city of Mumbai, we needed a rest and went on a holiday to the Indian part of Kashmir. We had been on the road for three days when we finally reached Srinagar on the border of the Himalayas and checked in to a stationary wooden houseboat on Lake Srinagar. Here we ran into the same problem as in Mumbai—four girls sharing a room with only two beds. I was drained and thought it was only fair if we took turns sleeping on the floor, and so I placed my bag on one of the beds. Then this woman, with what I perceived as sarcasm, said, "Why don't you and your friend sleep on the floor since you like being close?" I asked her what exactly she was driving at. The moment she brought the accusation, indicating that I was having what she called a 'lesbian-like' relationship with one of the team members, I was dumbfounded and felt as if a dagger had penetrated my heart.

The accusation impacted me so much because it happened in a Christian setting where sex outside marriage was looked upon as sinful, and same-sex all the more so. Furthermore, I wasn't prepared for such a response because I was normally well-liked and by default a very trusting person. At that moment I lost my innocent trust in people. The truth is that I was preoccupied with spiritual issues of life and thought of sex and physical needs as something that opposed spirituality. Consequently, I never paid much attention to my physical needs. I was probably a bit naive. Even if I had had boyfriends, I was without sexual experience, so how could I know for sure what my sexual identity was? I decided to ask the rest of the team if they had the same perception, which they all denied.

Over the past few months I had developed a beautiful friendship with one of the girls on the team. She was my best friend at the time and I cherished her a lot. She was going through a difficult time, and, being her friend and team leader, I tried to comfort her when she was upset or distressed. One of the ways was by being close to her—hugging her. According to Gary Chapman, the American author of *The Five Love Languages*, most people have one or two love languages that dominate—some people show love and affection by physical touch, while others prefer to communicate their love verbally or by giving a gift, helping out practically, or spending time with someone. In order to find out which love languages are our major ones, we can just look at our reaction to these different expressions. The act that makes us feel most cherished is likely to be our primary love language.

I know today that physical touch is my dominant love language, and from watching Mercedes relate to others I think hers was too. It seemed very natural for her to respond to others with some sort of physical touch, whether it was hugging, holding hands, kissing, or leaning toward someone. I can see quite a lot of myself in her expressive behavior, and today I know that it is a natural part of who I am. But as a young girl I wasn't aware of my love language, just as I didn't know that I had an existential wound from not receiving enough maternal tenderness and care, and that my brain was on an innate mission to cover such a need. Neither did I know about the hormone and neuro-chemical oxytocin, which is released when we are close to someone for thirty seconds or more. Oxytocin, also known as the bonding hormone, has a soothing effect on the nervous system by lowering the stress hormone cortisol, so closeness simply calmed me down. As a twenty-three-year-old girl with an enormous responsibility in a foreign land, I needed the closeness and the oxytocin to feel safe and counteract my stress. It wasn't sexual. Still the accusations haunted me for years.

I didn't tell anyone about the experience for many years afterward. I was still influenced by a religious mindset and

felt ashamed of the accusation, even though I had been innocent and was just being a normal, affectionate human being.

I had put a lot of effort into spiritual practices and had
probably become a spiritual role model to some. My expectations of myself and of what I believed others expected of me
stopped me from being open about it. But keeping it to myself fueled my shame, because shame thrives and prospers in
solitude. As the shame inside of me grew, so did the 'what if'
that had been planted about my sexual identity. When I married, at thirty-four, I was, as Mercedes put it, still 'a good girl,'
without sexual experience. It took me many years before I
could even share with my husband what had happened.
When I finally did, I was met with much love and understanding. My shame disappeared like a popped soap bubble.

Twenty-five years after the episode had taken place, I
met the girl I had once been close to in India and asked her if
the accusations had had any consequences for her. It turned
out that it hadn't affected her at all; she hardly knew what I
was talking about. The reason it hit me so hard was that I felt
responsible because I was the leader and had far too high
expectations of myself, but most of all because it connected
me with my existential wound, my 'mother wound.' Someone
can hurt us only if there is a wound inside that can be triggered. When we are whole, we can say never mind and move
on, something I wasn't able to do at the time. We all have a
breaking point, and I had reached mine. It was as if a rubber
band inside of me had been stretched too far and had finally
snapped. I had gotten my first serious injury and concluded
that something was terribly wrong with me since I had failed
to make everyone happy. I was in a state of shock, and my
tiredness reached a new level. I started having trouble falling

asleep at night because my brain was replaying the situation, trying to find an explanation or solution. Young as I was, I already suffered from severe burnout.

A YEAR after the incident in India, my dad had surgery for a tumor in his stomach. It turned out to be malignant and too big to remove. He died unexpectedly from a heart attack only three days after he had been diagnosed. After his death, I realized how much stability he had brought to the family just by being there. I also understood that his life had not been easy either.

With my father gone, my responsibility in the family, and for my mum especially, increased. The exhaustion was so massive that I began to avoid people and social events. I would sometimes hide in the bathroom with the lights turned off to avoid people who were seeking my company. I don't imply I was a celebrity in any way, but I was often in the spotlight and always surrounded by people. I can understand how tiring it must have been for Mercedes to have a love affair with people and to always be accessible.

In spite of my tiredness, I still managed to pull myself through teaching college and subsequently worked as a teacher for many years. Later I built up a travel and a real estate agency from scratch. I still wonder sometimes how I managed to pull it all together. I finally saw a therapist when I was forty-seven. She said it was a miracle that I hadn't dropped dead from all the stress. She didn't understand how

I had coped for so long with my heavy symptoms either. I think I was running on will and optimism alone, or maybe I had become addicted to work.

Research has shown that there is a link between chronic stress and addictive behavior. Some people become alcoholics, drug addicts, shopaholics, or they develop other disorders as a way of suppressing their inner pain. I had become an extremely hard worker. I got a kick from getting results. Workaholism is probably the only addiction apart from exercise addiction that is looked upon as a virtue. Even though being a workaholic is like other addictions in that it uses something as a way of coping with or numbing feelings, it is socially acceptable. People who are addicted to work are seen as ambitious, which makes it very difficult to spot as a problem. But like other forms of addiction, workaholism can have significant health consequences and trigger psychosomatic symptoms, which is what happened to me.

I felt energized as long as I worked. If I was tired I would sometimes write a long to-do list and start working. I could just go on and on without having any breaks. When I slowed down or rested, I got an awful headache or felt dizzy. It was a bit like having a hangover. I later understood that I was leading a lifestyle fueled by adrenalin, which has the same effect on the nervous system as speed. Unbeknownst to me, what this meant was that I was racing faster and faster toward adrenal fatigue or chronic fatigue.

FORTUNATELY, POSITIVE things took place in my life too. In August 1998, my best friend got engaged. Over the past six years, we had been spending most of our spare time together, so it was hard for me to appreciate that I was about to lose her. I didn't know anyone I could see myself with and decided to make a move. So I signed up for a singles party close to where I lived, and on August 29, 1998, a late summer evening, I embarked in my old red Audi and headed for my future.

The evening started with dinner, and I was sitting next to a gigantic, good-looking guy. He was a mechanical engineer and had been traveling all over the world, just like myself. We started chatting, and I immediately detected the uniqueness in his DNA. He appeared to me as a warm, sincere, and caring person with humor and intelligence that appealed to me. The feeling I got from sitting next to him was the feeling of finally reaching home after a long journey. I felt safe and in good company, and, after only one hour, I knew he was the man for me. When he asked me if I was interested in seeing him again, I had no hesitations and asked him if he wanted to see my car, a pickup line just to get a chance to be with him on my own. My car was twenty-five years old, the finish had faded, and I had painted it with spray, the entire car, all by myself. It is fair to say that it looked as if it had been tie dyed. Seeing it, he said, "I am a motor mechanic too, by the way."

I completely forgot I had promised someone a lift back because I was so excited. After six weeks, he proposed, and we got married only eight months after we had met. None of us doubted that we were meant for each other.

When we met, I was working as a teacher, and my future husband was working as an engineer, but we wanted more control in our lives. We were both worn out from life's events when we met, so we hoped to create a life outside the labor market that was less stressful. Shortly after we got married we started a travel agency and a real estate agency without having any experience in being self-employed. It was incredibly hard work, but we were doing quite well until the financial crisis reached Europe in 2008. When it did, we came under severe financial pressure and were struggling to keep our heads above water. We had already closed the travel agency due to the competition from the Internet and relied totally on our real estate agency. We had specialized in exquisite properties and had a monopoly on sales to Danish clients for the high-end Miami-based estate company, Fisher Island, which was constructing one of the most luxurious resorts in Costa del Sol, Spain. This prestigious project got us in contact with some of the richest investors in Denmark. One of our VIP clients wanted to buy a luxurious villa, and if we managed to sell the mansion, our commission would equal one full year of income for both of us, which meant we could avoid selling our house. There was a lot at stake for us, so naturally we were relieved when our clients, three days after they had viewed the property, confirmed that they wanted to buy. After their confirmation, we spent five weeks working with Spanish architects on some adjustments before the buyers returned to sign the purchase agreement.

The clients came back a second time to sign the contract. Everything seemed fine, but minutes before signing it, they unexpectedly pulled back. My heart started to beat faster. My mouth went dry, and I was swept off my feet, speechless. All I could think of was how we would manage to get through financially now. I was overcome with fear about the future and felt life had let me down, or, as Mercedes put it, that God had forsaken me. If I had been able to trust that life would work out for the best through anything that happened to us, I wouldn't have been run over by fear the way I was. Just like Mercedes didn't know beforehand that exile would open new doors for her and expand her career and her impact, I had no idea that our client had done us a tremendous favor; it would take me five years to comprehend that it was a gift in disguise.

The first challenge was to get back to Denmark as we didn't have money to fill the car with petrol for the three-thousand-kilometer journey. Luckily a good friend helped us out with a loan, so we packed the car and headed north. We didn't speak much—our minds were still processing what had happened. It was early spring in Spain. To our left, the slopes of Sierra Nevada were still dotted with snow, while to our right, orchards of almond and citrus trees were blossoming with hope, but our hope was gone.

We reached home on a chilly, foggy February morning and started almost immediately to empty the attic and pack things into boxes, desperate to sell our house fast before we were forced to sell it at a foreclosure auction. But it took us one and a half years before we could. Meanwhile, house prices dropped, and we ended up with a debt we didn't know how to pay off. We were willing to take up any job we could get. I got a job as a sales agent for Camel, Rodania, Mondaine, and Luminox watches. I visited all the goldsmiths in Jutland, the largest part of Denmark, only to realize that the crisis had affected the goldsmiths as well. No one wanted to buy new supplies before they had sold what they had in stock. I was on a commission and had to pay for the petrol myself. My commissions just added up to my expenses for petrol, so I ended up working for four months without any real income. My husband had started to bring out newspapers, but after three months he hadn't been paid any salary. Something fishy was going on. We lived close to the storehouse, and one evening we saw it go up in flames. It turned out that my husband's employer had attempted to commit insurance fraud and was sentenced to prison, charged with the torching of the building. The company closed, and my husband was never paid.

I managed to get a part-time job as a receptionist at a conference center, but besides that, we hardly had any income for almost three years. Denmark is known for having a good social service, but it didn't apply to people with their own business like us. We hung on to our company as we still had a few big investors wanting to buy luxurious properties. When we read in the papers that a client, one of the biggest investors in Denmark, had gone bankrupt, we finally decided to close down. We were forced to take out loans, but in the long run we couldn't take on more debt. We didn't have money for the basics, such as food and medical care. I didn't buy bones without meat from the market, like Mercedes had done, but I would buy food with the last date of expiration to get it cheap, and I searched the house for coins or things to sell before I would go shopping. Only a few people knew about our situation, but those who did supported us and would show up on our doorstep with boxes of food. For at least two years we lived largely on donations from friends and family. It was a touching experience, even though receiving, mostly from people who didn't have a significant financial buffer, wasn't always easy. I can relate to Mercedes' experience of feeling deeply moved by the solidarity her fellow artists showed her when she was alone with Fabián, struggling financially after her divorce from Oscar Matus.

We were in a vulnerable situation indeed. I woke up at night with my heart beating fast and couldn't go back to sleep. I was worried about what would become of us if the house sale dragged on. To cope, I had to focus on the present moment and thank life just for being alive, as Mercedes once put it. I felt cornered, like the story of the monk who went out for a walk in the jungle and was chased by a hungry tiger who forced the monk to climb down the wall of a canyon hanging on to a rope. Halfway down he discovered the rope wasn't long enough and he would be killed instantly by the jagged rocks at the bottom if he jumped. Above him, the tiger was still waiting, eager to get its lunch. While the monk was trying to decide about his next move, he saw two little mice gnawing at the rope and realized he was trapped. Then he spotted a strawberry growing out from a small crack in the wall of the canyon, only an arm's length away from him. He reached out for it, picked it, ate it, and said, "This is the best strawberry I have ever eaten in my entire life." I couldn't solve our situation either, but I started to eat lots of straw-berries.

THE STRESS we went through affected my husband too, but we reacted differently to the pressure: my husband became emotionally paralyzed, and I became hyperactive. It would have been easy for us to blame each other for doing too much or too little. Instead, we spent a lot of time talking about how the situation affected us. We began to understand that there was a direct correlation between how we reacted now and to how we tried to survive in our childhood. We also realized that our different reactions triggered something in each of us. The more paralyzed my husband was, the more I tried to fix things, and the more I tried to fix things, the more he became stuck. Looking back, we saw how our afflictions pushed us toward personal wholeness and strengthened our relationship as new understanding about ourselves and each other emerged. It became an opportunity for us to listen attentively and develop our empathy. Without empathy, we could easily have gone wrong with each other. Instead, we learned how two people can be in the same situation, reach different conclusions, and react differently without one part being either right or wrong simply because of how we viewed things. Understanding each other's narratives and which glasses each of us was seeing things through helped us to support each other. It sparked our love, and we avoided arguing and blaming each other, just as the spiritual leader Thích Nhất Hạnh puts it so beautifully:

"When you plant lettuce, if it does not grow well, you don't blame the lettuce. You look for reasons it is not doing well. It may need fertilizer, or more water, or less sun. You never blame the lettuce. Yet if we have problems with our friends or family, we blame the other person. But if we know how to take care of them, they will grow well, like the lettuce. Blaming has no positive effect at all, nor does trying to persuade using reason and argument. That is my experience. No blame, no reasoning, no argument, just understanding. If you understand, and you show that you understand, you can love, and the situation will change."

IN 2010, after closing our companies, I was diagnosed with Chronic Fatigue. Like Mercedes, my health was damaged by a combination of excessive work, repressing my feelings, and the mental burdens I had carried throughout my life. I never received medical treatment, except for my sleeping disorder and my headaches. The feedback I got from medical specialists was that I was having a normal reaction to an abnormal life.

My husband's workability was affected too, and, based on interviews and tests, doctors and specialists concluded that neither of us were able to work and that there was no cure. As a result, we were both forced into early retirement, even though we were only in our forties. We felt stuck and couldn't see a way out. It was as if all doors had closed on us. Normally, I would have a plan B and C, but this time I couldn't work my way out, which was difficult for a problem solver like me. I was in a situation I couldn't fix, and it was scary to lose control of my life. Nevertheless, it was a relief to be given a pension, but accepting our condition involved enormous grief. What would happen to our dreams about moving to an exotic country and having financial freedom when we couldn't work anymore? And paying our debt didn't seem possible for a long time ahead.

The financial pressure on top of everything else knocked me over completely. I reached a point where I couldn't get my pulse up or tolerate the slightest amount of pressure or excitement without hangovers setting in. Strength was gone from my body, and my cognitive abilities were heavily affected from the chronic stress and elevated cortisol. I constantly suffered from severe headaches and was extremely sensitive to noise. I could only be with one person at a time, and I couldn't take part in a conversation if there was any noise from music or other people talking in the background. Having been a missionary, a teacher, and a sales agent, I had had so many people in my life that I became exceedingly tired just from being with other people, even the people I cherished the most. Sometimes I had to stop in the middle of a conversation to say I needed a break because my brain couldn't cope with more input. When I went shopping, I avoided the big supermarkets where I easily lost my sense of direction and I became exhausted just from looking after what I needed.

The worst of all the hangovers, though, was a feeling of not being present. I felt I was looking out at the world through a glass or that I was watching my life from outside, as if it were a movie. Just as denial had prevented Mercedes from facing her pain, my disassociation was a defense mechanism my brain came up with to distance me from my agony. Each time I went through a traumatic experience, I felt like I lost a bit of my connection with myself.

During this period, I didn't keep in touch with my mother. As the pressure on me had grown and I felt the consequences of my stressful lifestyle, I began to see how my childhood had influenced my adult life. The stressful environment I had grown up in because of my mother's illness and the lack of emotional support had led to the onset of my burnout, for which I blamed my mother. I felt she had made me carry burdens far too big for a child. I also understood what I had missed out on in my childhood and in my youth. It was an excruciating process, and I needed a time-out to grieve and get my anger out.

I was about to lose my future as well, and I was desperate to get my life back—and not the adrenaline-fueled life I knew. I needed to learn to live all over again. I needed to become a human being instead of a human *doing*. For too long I had overheard the small whisper from my soul that told me not to push myself so hard. I had been either too busy to hear it or simply too unprepared.

It was under these difficult circumstances, physically, emotionally, and financially drained, that I heard about Mercedes Sosa for the first time. My encounter with her became the catalyst for my journey back to life. As Leonard Cohen sings in the song, "Anthem," *There is a crack in everything; that is how the light gets in.* Mercedes Sosa became that beam of light that shone through my cracks.

My Healing Journey with Mercedes Sosa

O N OCTOBER 4, 2009, when her death was announced on the news, I caught my first glimpse of Mercedes Sosa. There was a very short sequence of her singing "Gracias a la vida" at an acoustic concert in Switzerland in 1980. The video clip was less than a minute long, but enough to stir my curiosity. I simply had to find out more about this woman. I went straight to my computer to look her up online. The next day I got an email from a lovely lady I had met in a cottage on a holiday in Austria three months before. What she wrote me stirred my curiosity further:

"Yesterday Mercedes Sosa, an Argentine singer, died. Her depth, her honesty, her belief reminds me of you! I deeply feel that this world is losing such a powerful, brave, and honest woman. I really hope this energy will last on this planet, or maybe it can grow."

The first thing that struck me about Mercedes was her authenticity. I could sense that she was a person of tremendous integrity. What she expressed seemed to be in complete accordance with who she was. I could feel love flowing out of her, and she touched something deep inside of me. Tears began running down my cheeks as I watched her and listened to her songs. I was especially drawn to her eyes. I had to freeze the computer screen in order to watch her expression closely. More tears came. I felt she was looking straight at me, and with such tenderness. It reminded me of how a good friend of mine, Pauline Skeates, a psychotherapist from New Zealand and the founder of Insight Focused Therapy, had once looked at me on a holiday in Budapest.

On that particular evening, we were sitting having dinner at the famous Hotel Gellert, enjoying the view over the city with the Danube river winding through. We were just hanging out and having a good time after completing a seminar for psychology students in Romania. As I was talking, the look in my friend's eyes suddenly became very intense. I felt she was looking at me with admiration, so I got a bit embarrassed and turned my face away. Then she asked me to hold her gaze, and, with eyes full of compassion, she told me that she was just mirroring back to me what she saw in me. She had in effect recognized my existential wound and offered me what my mother had not been able to. It was a beautiful experience, but it also opened up a deep grief. I felt a need for my friend to keep watching me in this way, but since she lived on the opposite side of the world, it wasn't possible. With Mercedes Sosa, I got access to being mirrored any time I needed it and for as long as I needed it. Her gaze told me, "I see you, and in my eyes you are wonderful."

Feeling what it was like to be seen for who I was was both hurtful and healing at the same time. I had found a way to give the little girl within me all the love and care she needed and to become who I would have been if I had had this loving attention in my childhood.

AFTER A while, I realized that Mercedes Sosa had a soothing effect on my nervous system, which had been overloaded with chronic stress since my childhood. Stress is not always a bad thing, as it can help us to achieve more, increasing our energy and our focus, but constantly living with high levels of the stress hormones adrenaline and cortisol cause the body's stress response, fight or flight, to be always switched on. Over time, it can cause immense damage to both our body and our brain. Cortisol literally consumes the brain and makes it shrink. It affects three areas in our brain: the hippocampus, the prefrontal cortex, and the amygdala. As a result, our memory, learning ability, and stress control are impaired as well as our decision making, our judgment, and our social interactions. Meanwhile, the neural connections in the brain's fear center, the amygdala, increase. It is not busyness or acute danger alone that can cause the stress hormones to rise. If our environment and relationships are dysfunctional and full of tension, they induce us always to be on guard. For a child to grow up with parents who are not getting along, or with a parent's illness, as I did, leads to constant stress.

Interestingly, research has revealed that there is a connection between how well we handle stressful situations and with the extent of nurture we receive in early childhood. An experiment with rats has shown that the amount of nurturing a mother rat gave its newborn baby was key to how that baby responded to stress later in life. The baby of a nurturing mother was less sensitive to stress because its brain developed more cortisol receptors, which toned down the stress response. On the contrary, baby rats of neglecting mothers became more sensitive to stress throughout their life because their genes were affected. The bad news is that the experiment shows that reactions to stress were passed down from one single mother to many generations of rats without these babies being exposed to stress themselves, but the good news is that if the neglecting mother was swapped with a nurturing mother, the sensitivity to stress in the baby rat was reversed.[48] Research has shown that the sensitivity to stress can be reversed in humans too, and I believe that being mentally nurtured by Mercedes for a while somehow was part of a reversing process.

AFTER DISCOVERING Mercedes Sosa, I'd sit down daily and practice mindfulness, a meditation form I had learned from my friend in New Zealand. I'd sit quietly and breathe deeply in and out without planning for anything to happen; I was merely paying attention to the present moment and to what was going on in my mind.

Scientists have studied the brains of people who have practiced mindful meditation twenty-seven minutes a day for eight weeks. They found that the practice increases the density of the prefrontal cortex, which is responsible for calming down our instinctive emotional responses, such as fear, and decreases the size of the amygdala, the center of the brain's fight-or-flight response. Furthermore, mindfulness also causes the stress hormone cortisol to decrease, and the neurotransmitter, GABA, that works as a handbrake, slowing down a busy brain, to increase. It explains the increased sense of peace and alleviation caused by meditation.

I almost always listened to a song by Mercedes while meditating, and sometimes memories came to my awareness unbidden. When unpleasant or unsolved situations from my childhood emerged, I used my imagination to picture what the situation would have been like if Mercedes had been there with me. This became a tool that I used to balm some of the pain stored up inside of me. I would often find an expression on Mercedes' face that I needed for a specific moment. Then I would freeze the computer screen and talk to her.

Mindfulness is not only about being present in the moment; it is also about being present in a compassionate and nonjudgmental way. Spontaneously, I began to stroke my face with my hands in long, slow movements that followed the rhythm of my breathing. Being kind and gentle toward myself and touching my skin in a loving way enabled me to connect with myself and feel more present as it caused the release of oxytocin in my body. Having a loving and accepting attitude toward myself became a part of my daily meditation practice and one of the keys to my recovery.

It appears to me that Mercedes knew how to be mindful and compassionate toward herself. She would often place her hand over her heart or chest while singing with her eyes closed, as if she was blessing herself and being kind to herself. She was probably just following her intuition in the same way as I did.

Showing kindness has been found to be a soothing action, countering the effects of stress, whether the kindness is directed toward someone else or shown to oneself. Dr. Anna M. Cabeca, a board-certified gynecologist and obstetrician and an expert in women's health in the United States, describes the relationship between oxytocin and cortisol as two kids on a seesaw. "When one goes up, the other is forced to go down,"[49] she says. This is exactly what I experienced. When I meditated with a loving and caring attitude toward myself, it gave me a sense of calm, and tears of relief would flow down my face as I allowed a memory to emerge without judging it or trying to make it go away. I travelled backward through my childhood and up until the time I became a teenager. With the help of mindfulness and imagination, Mercedes and I rewrote the stories together in a way that diminished the impact of the traumas. Afterward, I wrote down these memories and imagined situations. Here are three entries that illustrate what I shared with Mercedes as I pictured her right next to me:

One

I am eight years old. My mum got upset and took off and I am afraid. When will she come back? Have I done anything wrong? What can I do to please her when she gets back? How can I make her happy? I am crying on the inside but don't want to show my dad. He probably won't know how to handle it if I begin to cry. I am holding back my tears while he is reading me a fairy tale, but I don't listen. I am somewhere else, and all I feel is fear and pain. We decide to make a little surprise for Mum; maybe that will make her happy when she gets back. "Mercedes, please hold me and tell me that things will be okay. Take me with you. Take me out of here. Tell me that it is okay to cry."

Two

I am twelve. We are sitting at the dinner table. I am trying to create a good atmosphere and get the talking going, but I am so tense because I don't know how this meal will turn out. I already sense the tension in the room. Will my mother burst out and leave the table and lock herself up in the bedroom? If she does, how do I get her to open the door? I am standing in front of the locked door, trying to get in contact with her, but there is only silence. If only she would speak to me. I call out to her, but she is not talking back. I go for a walk and feel so lonely. If only I could talk to someone, but I don't want anybody to know that my mother is having problems. It is a secret. Now

167

you are here with me. I don't have to carry the burden alone and sharing the secret with you brings relief."

Three

I am seven. It is my first day at school. I am the last pupil out of maybe a hundred children to be called to the class. I think no one wants me. I don't know my surname starts with one of the last letters of the alphabet and that we are called out alphabetically. Mercedes comes up to me and stands next to me. She takes my hand in that big hall among all those people. "Being the last pupil to be called to class has nothing to do with no one wanting you. You are a precious little girl who is very special," she assures me.

After each journey back to my childhood, I asked Mercedes to support me and to wrap her arms around me as I continued my recovery toward wholeness. Expressing my needs and standing by them, something I never did as a child, had a healing effect in itself. I pictured how Mercedes would respond to me, what she would say to me, how she would look at me, comfort me, and dry my tears. My childhood fear and loneliness were replaced with relief and peace.

But how was I able to sense Mercedes Sosa's essence and use it for my inner healing and envision a relationship with her? I decided to do some research to understand why healing was taking place and discovered the answer in neuroscience. In recent years, neuroscientists have been exploring the way that humans share a system of mirror neurons. Mirror neurons were discovered by coincidence in 1990 by an experimenter who studied the brains of monkeys in his lab. One day he returned to his lab from lunch while eating an ice cream, when he noticed that the brain of a monkey already set up for a test would fire exactly in the same way as if the monkey was eating the ice cream itself.

This applies to the human brain as well, and it is the mirror neurons that make us able to identify with what other people are feeling and going through; without them we couldn't show empathy. Daniel Siegel, a professor of clinical psychiatry at the UCLA School of Medicine and a pioneer in the field of *interpersonal neurobiology*, defines how mirror neurons make it possible for us to connect with others. When someone communicates with us, the neurons can fire and dissolve the border between us and others so we can understand the mind state of another person and develop empathy. The mirror neurons ". . . automatically and spontaneously pick up information about the intentions and feelings of those around us, creating emotional resonance and behavioral imitation as they connect our internal state with those around us, even without the participation of our conscious mind,"[50] Siegel writes.

This finding is supported by the work of Dr. Stephen Porges of the University of Illinois at Chicago on the social engagement system (SES). Porges has examined the way attachment works between individuals. He clarifies how looking into the face of another person has a huge effect on us. He explains that a "neuroception of safety" is communicated by way of the vagus nerve. The vagus nerve is intimately connected with our compassionate response. It is in charge of our inner nerve center—the parasympathetic nervous system—and works like a walkie-talkie that sends out messages via electric impulses from our gut to our brain about how we are feeling. It is also responsible for controlling our heart rate and communicates with our face muscles, particularly the muscles around our mouth and our eyes. The social engagement system works automatically and picks up signals from others, such as body language, voice quality, and facial expressions. On a deep, unconscious level, we have the ability to discern whether a smile is genuine or not and whether we can allow ourselves to be safe enough to connect with another person. When we do, the release of oxytocin deepens the experience.

If the social engagement system likes what it sees and hears, it calms us. Therapist and airline captain Tom Bunn actively uses the social engagement system when he works with fearful fliers. He asks his clients to tap into a memory where someone's facial expression has caused the social engagement system to actively control anxiety. He then tells his clients to link the face of that person to the entire flight process, from taking off to landing. When the various moments of flight are linked to vivid memories of a person's face and the signals are sent to the social engagement system, it calms down the stress response and helps control anxiety.[51] Without knowing it, I was intuitively using Mercedes' facial expressions to calm me in a similar way.

These human mechanisms, the mirror neurons and the social engagement system, enable us to see the innate goodness in another person, and science shows that practicing loving kindness and compassion increases our well-being because it alters the circuits in the left side of the prefrontal cortex, which is associated with positive feelings. I was developing empathy and practicing loving kindness as I focused my attention on the beauty, love, and authenticity I saw in Mercedes Sosa, and thanks to the social engagement system, my encounter with her became a mind-blowing and mind-altering experience.

THE MYSTERY of how Mercedes could have such a nourishing effect on my nervous system is made clear by Siegel in his book *Mindsight*, where he describes how "our receptivity, our experience of being safe and seen, counteracts the reactive fight-flight-freeze survival reflex."[51] My survival reflex had been switched on for years, and Mercedes caused it to be switched off by making me feel safe and seen, even though it happened through a computer screen. A fictive relationship, as I had with Mercedes Sosa, can't replace real-life relationships, but in the context of healing my 'mother wound,' it worked wonders because the brain doesn't differentiate between what is real and what is perceived. Sometimes our brain perceives a threat and sets us up to fight or flight, even though there's no danger. This inbuilt survival response happens automatically, whether the danger is real or not—our brain just wants to keep us safe, which explains why a shadow that looks like a large dog may be as frightening as an actual large dog to someone who has been bitten by a dog.

Like mindfulness, our imagination can stimulate our brains and our bodies. Just thinking about a lemon can create the same sensations and produce saliva as if we were eating a lemon. If we use our imagination to think about what can go wrong, like failing an exam, for example, it can cause stomach ache and anxiety. Because the brain is set up to look out for danger, worrying and anxious thoughts tend to stick to us more easily than positive thoughts. The good news is that we can use our imagination deliberately to picture something positive and take advantage of the fact that the brain can be triggered into believing that something is real. Imagining Mercedes Sosa as a compassionate mother created a positive response that soothed me both physically and emotionally.

The reason Mercedes Sosa was a perfect imaginary figure to me was first of all because she was a woman who fitted the role as a mother perfectly. She radiated compassion, kindness, and empathy which made me feel nurtured and cared for. Her being someone who had known pain and suffering yet had survived provided me with a feeling that she was able to identify with what I went through and gave me hope that I would overcome my difficulties too. In contrast to what I had experienced in my childhood, Mercedes was strong, and in my fictive relationship with her she would carry my burdens, keep me safe, and protect me. Her ability to embrace all sorts of people—be respectful and nonjudgmental—gave me the confidence to share my secrets with her without being shamed. I felt loved and accepted, receiving her joy and energy. Even if it was all happening in my imagination, my brain perceived the experience as real and my whole being responded with well-being.

Consequently, I could use my envisioned relationship to change the neural firing in the brain and thereby become free of repetitive, destructive patterns formed by my early relationships. Interpersonal neurobiology claims that healthy relationships are essential in our development, that it is important to take good care of our connections with others because positive relationships cause positive changes that initiate healing.

Far more than we are consciously aware of, our daily encounters with others shape our brains for good or ill because they work together with the mind and the brain as a whole and can shape the focus of our attention and what we envision. The brain is the physical substrate of the mind. Our mind regulates our brain and sends a flow of information emerging from our relationships to the nervous system. When our relationships are attuned, they enable the brain to function well and give the mind a deep sense of connection and well-being.[51]

My JOURNEY with Mercedes was taking place spontaneously and in private, but I also had one therapy session with Pauline Skeates, from New Zealand, which became key to my recovery. During our session, I pictured myself once again, this time as a very young girl getting ready to leave home. At first I was inside my home with all the tensions, but then I opened the front door, stepped outside, and started to walk away. I turned around and waved goodbye a couple of times and saw my home becoming smaller and smaller as I continued to move further and further away until I made a turn at a corner and couldn't see my home anymore. Then Pauline asked me to pick the girl up, keep her in my hands, and squeeze her to make her smaller so I could place her in my heart. With the girl symbolically inside of me, I began to speak to her and listen to her needs. I told her that I would take care of her, that she wouldn't have to worry about me or carry any burdens anymore. I was the adult, and I would make sure she would have her needs met, I assured her.

This became a turning point. I felt a change within immediately as the unnatural tie to my mother had been cut. From that day the sense that she had been living her life inside of me stopped, and I didn't feel guilty or sad on her behalf any more. The disassociation left me too, and I felt connected to myself again. When I returned from the session and watched myself in the mirror, I could see a sparkle of life in my eyes again.

Pauline advised me to keep talking to the girl within to affirm the change for at least three weeks in order to change my old habitual way of thinking by establishing new neural pathways. Neurons are cells that send signals to and from each other in the brain, and as the saying goes, "Neurons that fire together, wire together." There are one hundred billions of neurons in the brain and each neuron has thousands of connections with other neurons, which means there are trillions of neural connections in the brain. The more we keep thinking about the same thing, the stronger this connection in the brain becomes. As I continued to focus on my new perspective, new neural connections were formed, which eventually changed my perception of the past.

Mindfulness, refocusing, and imagination are powerful tools whereby we can take control of our attention and redesign the neural pathways of our brains, which is what rewriting our story is about. I believe everyone can rewrite their story by connecting with their little boy or little girl within. Rewriting one's story is not about denying anything; it is about acknowledging what it was really like to be in a certain situation and then bringing in a better one. If you become aware of things that happened to you in your childhood–things that are affecting your present life in a negative way–maybe you can use my experience as inspiration. Perhaps your brain will protect you from painful memories and make you think that your childhood was okay compared to others. But remember it is the threat or neglect your brain has perceived that matters. Try to be open and curious without forcing anything to happen and remain sensitive to what is the best road for you to take. If you can't think of someone who you can use as your imaginary parent, you can look for a photo of a person with an expression that triggers a positive response in you and use it in your healing process. If you can't find such a photo, try to picture yourself as a loving and caring adult and imagine what you would say to and do for your inner child in a certain situation.

MY WOUND was healing, but my health was so poor that for three years I wasn't able to do much. I forced myself to go for slow, short walks every day or to swim a little. I was hardly able to socialize. When I saw someone, it was one person at a time for no more than an hour. The only thing I could do without getting exhausted was listen to music, and mostly only acoustic music, which meant it was mostly only Mercedes' songs. I bought all her CDs and made music tracks on my computer of my favorites and used them as part of my meditations. I had a list for peace, hope, and comfort, and one for joy, strength, and energy. Some days it would be one particular song that I listened to over and over again. I spent hours every day listening to Mercedes' songs and found that music became my medicine. While I was listening, I also began drawing the portraits that you find throughout the book.

What music will have a healing effect for which individual will be different from person to person, but we can't overestimate the value of music for our well-being. It gives us a way to get in touch with our emotions, and a way to express them. Because it has an alleviating effect, it is now often used in hospitals to bring relief to patients. Scientists are still trying to figure out what's going on in our brains when we listen to music. Daniel Levitin, a prominent psychologist who studies the neuroscience of music at McGill University, in Montreal, has analyzed the rating of anxiety and cortisol in four hundred patients who listened to music before undergoing surgery. He found that the patients who listened to music had less anxiety and lower cortisol than people who used medicine.[52]

Another researcher, a postdoctoral candidate at Stanford University School of Medicine, Daniel Abrams, states that music triggers activity in the part of our brain that releases the feel-good chemical dopamine. When dopamine is released in the limbic system, it is associated with pleasure, but when it is released in the frontal lobes, it helps increase attention, planning, movement, and memory.[53] It's no wonder that music can affect our mood, trigger memories, and foster loving associations when applied with intention, like it happened to me.

I didn't know anything about all of this at the time of my healing process, of course. It just happened that way as I intuitively followed the road laid out before me. As I listened to Mercedes' songs, my body relaxed. The songs soothed my soul, and I felt a deep consolation within. Her voice made me feel that I was not only listening to music but to life itself in its essence. Mercedes knew very well that her voice had this effect on people. She once said in an interview, "I know what happens with my voice when I sing. My voice is used as consolation for many."[3]

Clearly it was the consolation and the healing that went out from her that caused many in her audience to cry and to relate to her as a mother figure. As we learned in part one, even Mercedes herself felt that she was being healed when she sang.

I HAD managed to undo my painful memories from my childhood, but I still suffered from one of my most traumatic experiences twenty-three years after it had happened. The trauma was not inflicted by my mother, but by the person who questioned my integrity when I was a team leader in India. What I was accused of was directly linked to my existential wound—my need of a mother's love. I wasn't aware of having an existential wound at that time, but today I understand the connection. I needed healing from that experience, and, again, I talked to Mercedes about it:

Mercedes, I have something else to tell you. Something happened in 1988 that hurt me deeply. At that time, I lost my innocent trust in people, my health, and my ability to sleep. I will invite you to be there with me on that houseboat at Lake Srinagar in Kashmir where it all happened. What would you do and say to me in that situation?

I see you there. As the words are spoken, you just look at me with such sympathy and understanding in your eyes. But I also see the pain in your eyes because you know that something is being destroyed deep inside me. Without saying anything, you stand and come toward me. In front of all the others, you bow down and kiss me on my forehead and on the cheeks. Then you whisper in my ear, "It is not true. Don't believe it. I know that what you need is the mother love you never received, and I am here with you to give it to you."

Then you draw me into your arms in a warm embrace. You promise to stay with me all night and for as long as I want. You sit by my bed and sing songs of comfort and healing to me. You tell me it is okay to need a mother, even now. "You can always come to me, no matter how old you get. You are the joy of my heart. Soak yourself in my love. Wrap it around you like a blanket to protect you from the disappointments of life," I hear you say.

Today I realize that you were there with me, although I didn't see you. But I invite you to be there for me now to heal my heart and my memory. You have convinced me that there was nothing wrong with me; I didn't do anything wrong. I just needed to be loved in the way I should have been loved as a little girl by my mother. Understanding this is setting me free.

Throughout my journey I often listened to the beautiful song "This is to Mother You," by Sinead O'Connor. The lyrics put words to the experience I had with Mercedes Sosa:

"This is to be with you
To hold you and to kiss you too
For when you need me I will do
What your own mother didn't do
Which is to mother you."

Through the compassionate eyes of Mercedes Sosa I had been mothered, mirrored, nurtured, and validated in a way that healed my existential wound.

The healing took place over four to five years, and in my last writing to her the difference in me is noticeable. Deep and lasting change had taken place in an unexpected and unusual way

Dear Mercedes,

It has been a long, tiring, and challenging journey for me. I am still feeling very exhausted, but you are helping me accept life as it is, and I don't feel I am a victim anymore. I am a survivor like you. You came to me in a unique way. I have not met you in person but I recognize you constantly. My heart has reached your heart. I know you and I feel you. You touched me strongly from the beginning. You played the deepest strings in me and woke me up. You taught me to live with courage as I allowed the intensity of your tenderness and compassion to heal me. You give me the strength to fight, to feel, to live and to love, and

I am embracing my history and everything I have been through in life. I am standing by who I am and the choices I have made. I feel no shame, and I throw myself into your arms, knowing that I am loved for who I am, confident that you are welcoming me as I am.

Conclusion

ERCEDES SOSA'S LIFE points out the importance of trusting our inner wisdom. When we listen to our inner voice, it can lead us to a more contended way of being and empower us to stand tall in the midst of the strong winds in life. Long before mindfulness and self-compassion became acknowledged in the Western world, Mercedes intuitively lived by these terms. Her outstanding ability to perform with an acute mind and impassioned precision shows that she was living in the present moment. Furthermore, she could manifest her true self without depending on affirmation from others because she had learned to be kind and compassionate toward herself.

If we haven't been seen and felt welcomed for who we are, and learned to be compassionate toward ourselves, we will most likely end up depending on the likes and dislikes of others. We may sacrifice our authenticity by not fully expressing ourselves. Who we are is far more important than our talent. Talent is expressed through *doing*, while DNA is expressed through *being*. Mercedes was aware of this. "There are things that are more important than the vocal cords. It's what you feel when you make a sound, feelings of love, of solidarity with others. It's not about technique. It's about what is inside," she explained in a phone interview with Don Heckman for LA Times in 1995.

Sosa obviously had a noteworthy, exquisite, and supreme talent that opened doors for her to influence politics and culture worldwide, but she also possessed the ability to connect with people in a way that was unprecedented by any other public figure in her time. Whether she was in the presence of presidents, with poor immigrants, children, or peasants, she was always respectful, attentive, and present. The real secret behind her impact was indeed her authenticity—the way she expressed her innate qualities.

It was most likely her upbringing in a loving and emotionally supportive family, paired with her willingness to be shaped by the opposition and suffering that she faced, that fostered her authenticity. However, those of us who haven't had a secure and loving childhood can still live authentic lives and come face to face with our past and embrace our little or much-wounded selves. We all have something unique within us that we must find a way to express, because even if we don't have any extraordinary talent, we can still make a positive difference to someone. When we reach out to someone the chance is that the love that flows through us will bring healing to us in the process as well.

Mercedes probably never heard about interpersonal neurobiology, but she must intuitively have sensed the healing power of love and connection. It was love that motivated her to speak up for those on the margins of society. She sang for people because she loved them and would often shout out to her audience, "No one can and no one should live without love."[54] To connect people with love was her mission, and she found strength in the love she received from others.

Only an authentic person who has overcome his or her fear of rejection can truly love others, and only a person who has come to terms with his or her imperfection and humanity is capable of receiving love. We only experience to be fully loved to the extent that we are willing to be fully seen. But it takes much courage to step out of our hiding and say, "Here I am," because it makes us vulnerable. Vulnerability is the price we must pay for being loved and becoming authentic. If we protect ourselves from being hurt, we also cut ourselves off from the essence of the human experience, from love, intimacy, and connection. Without vulnerability, we can't make a genuine connection with each other and know what it is like to be welcomed for who we are.

No one can do the inward journey toward wholeness for us, but we all do better with a little help from someone who supports us on the journey and who loves us for who we are. As we move on toward authenticity, nurture our capacity for empathy, and engage in the neural waltz that connects us to each other, we can become the mirror that reflects to someone the goodness and beauty we see in him or her, just like Mercedes did. As we have witnessed, she knew how to embrace the unexpected and the odd, whether it was an addict, a person with Down syndrome, noisy teenagers, or a person with HIV. Her ability to see the beauty in people and welcome them made her appear mysterious, probably because the effect of such loving attention is truly powerful for someone who hasn't met it before.

A friend once told me a sweet little story about her two-year-old daughter. One morning the daughter woke the parents up early by entering their bedroom with her arms spread out wide while confidently announcing, "Here I am!" What a wonderful way to be in this world, confident of who we are, expecting to be welcomed for who we are. We all need a place where we know we are welcome. This is what Mercedes did to so many when she was alive, and it is what she did to me after her death. It was her voice that opened the way for her, but it was her ability to connect with people with love by saying, "I see you. You are wonderful," that made her so influential.

Mercedes Sosa deserves to go down in history as a world legend. Standing out by being a woman, Sosa's impact goes far beyond politics. Her heart of motherhood reaches out to all of us with healing, compassion, and validation. Her voice still reaches the human soul. It goes behind all facades and finds the place where we are all just human beings. She is not only the voice of Latin America, she is the voice of the most beautiful and profound feeling in the world - LOVE! She is the voice of the humble, of those who suffer, of those who are forgotten. Always in our hearts, Mercedes gives us strength to move forward with the dream of a more just world full of hope.

Epilogue

A RGENTINA IS STILL struggling with the ghosts of the past. On August 1, 2017, Santiago Maldonado, a twenty-eight-year-old fine arts graduate and tattoo artist, went missing at an indigenous-rights demonstration in Patagonia, where the Mapuche people are claiming their ancestral right to a small piece of land owned by Benetton, the Italian clothing retailer. When security forces showed up and fired lead and rubber bullets at the protesters, some of the protesters jumped into the Chubut River to escape. Santiago, who couldn't swim, was clinging to a tree and detained by the police, a witness reported. The national security minister denied that the police were involved, and the police denied detaining Santiago.

The disappearance led to massive protests across the country. The Argentines protested on social media and protests were also held in coordination with the Grandmothers of Plaza de Mayo's weekly march to demand memory, truth, and justice in the name of their disappeared children during the dictatorship. "We've gone back in time forty years. I can't accept it," said Rosa Tarlovsky de Roisinblit, 98, the vice president of the Grandmothers of Plaza de Mayo.

Cristina Fernández de Kirchner, who is eyeing a return to the presidency in 2019, has been fiercely critical of the government's response to Maldonado's disappearance, saying that she no longer believed there was rule of law in Argentina.

Maldonado has become a symbol for various conflicts, from indigenous rights to government repression, and has revived bitter memories of Argentina's 1976-83 military dictatorship. His disappearance has put pressure on the centre-right government of President Mauricio Macri, which has tried to downplay the crimes of Argentina's dictatorship. When asked by a journalist from an Argentine newspaper whether he thought that the number of disappeared during the dictatorship was thirty thousand, Macri responded: "I have no idea. If there were nine thousand or thirty thousand, I think it's a discussion that makes no sense."

Santiago's body was found after seventy-eight days in the Chubut River. No one has been held responsible for the crime, and the only police officer indicted got promoted by the security ministry. In December 2017 a report published by The Coordinator Against Police and Institutional Repression stated that Argentina is going through the most violent repressive peak since 1983. Had Mercedes Sosa still been alive, I believe she would have been crying for Argentina, speaking up for injustice, singing hope into people's despair, and uniting and comforting them with a warm embrace.

AFTER A PERIOD of separation, my mother and I restored our relationship. When I addressed her with my troublesome childhood, she was first in denial and felt sorry for herself, but when she realized how serious my health condition was, she became remorseful and asked for forgiveness. She also began thanking me for all the things I had done for her over the years. I had healed already, so I could tell her that I understood how difficult life with three children had been for her when she hardly slept at all. I told her I knew she had done her best and that she had given me good things in life too. I was now able to see the gift in everything that I had been through and told her that it was a part of the journey I had to go through in order to become the person I am.

Today my mother is eighty-two years old. In spite of her adversities, she has managed to love life and hang onto it. But just before publishing this book she suddenly became very ill and couldn't take care of herself anymore. I spent three months looking after her before settling her into an eldercare home. At first the thought of getting back into the old role of taking responsibility for her again made me uncomfortable, but, seeing her condition, caring came to me naturally. This unexpected opportunity to show her my love and compassion became a beautiful healing experience. In the midst of her weakness she was attentive, grateful, and loving. I felt she needed to catch up on showing me affection and I let her. She would cry and say, "I wasn't good to you as a child, but I was ill." These three months with my mother has proved that the healing I have shared with you really has taken place because otherwise I couldn't have handled the situation. There isn't any hurt left at all and I admire and respect my mother because she managed to change in old age, and I am proud of her.

I hold no resentment against the woman on my team in India. I met her on multiple occasions afterward, and she admitted having been "a little too hard on me." It took me more than twenty-five years to free myself from the words, but today I can talk about it without feeling embarrassed. The insinuation wouldn't have the same power to hurt me today as I don't see sexual orientation as a big issue anymore. I am not allowing class, age, race, religion, sexuality, or even a diagnosis to define who I am, and I try not to pigeonhole others with these limiting definitions either. The gift of my painful experience is that it gave me an opportunity to become aware of my existential wound so it could heal. I am not hurting inside, and I am no longer driven by a need to be special. My healing process has ended for now, and if anything aggravates the wound in the future, I know what it is and how to take care of it. In the process, I managed to liberate myself from the dualistic way of thinking, and nowadays I am not as hard on myself. I appreciate my body, listen to it, and treat it better than I used to. The more compassionate I have become toward myself, the easier it is for me to embrace others.

My health is still not as good as I would like it to be, but it has improved. I am learning to live a quieter life without exposing myself to stress or pressure. I try to focus on what I *can* do instead of what I *can't* do and. I have learned to look for the gift hidden within my limitations. I feel I have gotten some of my life back, albeit in a different form.

A hard thing about living with a chronic fatigue-related disease is that others can't see it unless they know me well. I tend to underplay how tired I actually am, and I don't like to look as tired as I sometimes feel. It has taught me that it is important to explain to others how much I can handle and why I do things the way I do to avoid misunderstandings.

Sometimes I need the people closest to me to support me in taking better care of myself and tell the always lurking workaholic to back off. I haven't come across anyone who has recovered from chronic fatigue, which for some time was quite disillusioning. But as I look back at my process I can see progress. Recovery is taking place over time. I still can't get my pulse up for long periods, and the best way to stay fit is to swim, especially snorkeling, which requires deep breathing, like in meditation. I was expecting a setback after the hard work of moving my mother to the eldercare home, but the opposite happened. My health suddenly improved. I became able to sleep without sleeping pills for the first time in twenty-five years. I began to feel more energized and even started to ride a mountain bike moderately. My ability to socialize improved too. I'm still trying to understand what happened and believe there might be a connection to the final healing that took place in my relation to my mother. My story shows that no matter how low you are, it is important not to lose hope because some degree of recovery is possible over time.

One of the most amazing things I have discovered is that healing accelerates within healthy relationships where there is a constant flow of loving kindness and generosity. Focusing on the good I see in those around me and being able to reach out to someone I care about, whether it is emotionally or financially, has boosted my well-being—my feeling of happiness and purpose in life. Out of love, I have been motivated to do things I thought I was too tired ever to do again. Writing this book is a product of such a process. My affection for Mercedes Sosa energized me with a hope that either Mercedes' story or my journey would inspire and bring hope to others. I never thought I was capable of accomplishing this, and it has taken almost nine years to complete it, but what a joyful journey it has been—most of the time.

I am still passionate about Mercedes Sosa and her music, and I hope to be able to visit Argentina one day. I love listening to Latin American music, and I have added artists like Soledad Pastorutti, León Gieco, Patricia Sosa, Lila Downs, Jorge Drexler, and Pablo Milanés to my list of favorite Latin American singers.

My husband and I have been together for nineteen years and we are now both in early retirement, and continuing to pay off the debts from the sale of our house and years without income. The only possible way we could continue to do that while being on a pension was by lowering our living expenses. After some research, it seemed that Turkey was the best country to choose for this. We moved to a resort town on the Aegean coast in 2012 and are still living there as I write. When there was nothing we could do to pursue our dream, amazingly the dream came to us when we finally threw in the towel. A great lesson in daring to let go and trust life.

A year after we had moved to Turkey, something amazing happened, which was also a continuation of my journey with Mercedes Sosa.

One day in August 2013, I was on my way back from the beach when I passed by a small shop which I passed by every day. This particular day I spotted a beautiful turquoise batik dress that was hanging outside. Turquoise being my favorite color at the time, I decided to stop and try it on. Up to that time we had met only two English-speaking Turkish people, so when the lady in the shop approached me and I realized she spoke English quite well, I was surprised and overjoyed.

I was a little stunned too because she looked almost exactly like Mercedes Sosa at a young age. She was a small exotic-looking woman with long black hair and intense dark eyes. Furthermore, as the social engagement system set in, I immediately recognized that her heart attitude, her essence, was similar to Mercedes Sosa's. Naturally I couldn't help but ask her the same question I had asked everybody on my way the past four years, though I never got an affirmative answer. I asked, "Do you know Mercedes Sosa?"

Her answer made my heart jump. "Of course I know her. I love her!"

When I told her I was writing a book about Mercedes Sosa, she got excited and said she wanted to read it and even sell it in her shop. She also told me she had been working in the book industry in Turkey most of her life and was keen on translating the book into Turkish. I wasn't finished when we met, but meeting her encouraged me to do so and get it published.

This meeting was the beginning of a new and beautiful friendship. Connecting with her in a real-life friendship speeded up my recovery. She became my 'Turkish Miracle,' my 'Mini Sosa,' and my second darling. Every time I see her I conclude that life never let me down.

Serhan, my 'Turkish Miracle,' and Sosa look-alike

Interview

Luis Plaza Ibarra - Close friend

What does Mercedes Sosa mean to you?
Mercedes Sosa was a part of my daily life and my history. Growing up in Chile under a dictatorship where music by "protesting artists" was completely forbidden, Mercedes Sosa became an important person who explained how people die and disappear under oppression. Through her songs and her lyrics she gave me a feeling of hope in the midst of the terrible things that took place. Being a musician myself it was a delight to listen to her.

How has she influenced your life?
Mercedes inspired me to always do my best and to be responsible in every way, culturally as well as musically. She taught me that no one becomes great without studying and continuing to improve.

What is the most important thing you have learned from her?
Mercedes always gave an impression of warmth and human compassion. She didn't behave as a diva. If you are great you don't have to show off or prove yourself to anyone. True greatness is showing respect for everyone. Mercedes was the epitome of greatness. She also taught me to work for a united Latin America where all brothers are equal.

Which episode from the years you spent with her has made the biggest impact on you?

It was when Mercedes, during the last tour in Germany in 2008, shared all the stories behind the recordings with us as we travelled together for two weeks in a minibus. To hear everything "live" was really amazing!

Can you mention a funny episode from your time together?

There are many, but right now I can think of one episode. It was after a concert and we had just got on the minibus where the radio was playing one of her best known songs internationally. Mercedes broke out, saying, "Shut that music off, for heaven's sake. I have been singing it for fifty years, and I don't want to listen to it anymore." The next time the audience requested her to sing this particular song, she did it very professionally, but I knew how she felt about it.

What where the highlights in her life professionally and privately the last eight years of her life?

Professionally the highlights were the tours in Italy, Spain, and Germany, which were the countries she felt at home in during her time in exile. Israel was a highlight as well. All her concerts were sold out and Mercedes always said, "They haven't forgotten me. They still love me." To feel the love from her audience was her strength in life.

The work with her farewell CD, *Cantora* was important too. She didn't live long enough to know that it won a Grammy, but she had the joy of knowing it was nominated. During our tour through Germany she spent a lot of time revising her repertoire. She still had high expectations for herself and said, "I have to do it well. The recording will be out there forever." At a personal level the highlight was being with her best friends. Even if she was weak she always found energy and time to enjoy their company.

How did she handle her illness when she was touring?
She handled it by more or less repressing it. She tried to keep busy with her repertoire and gave herself to her work fully. She didn't talk about her illness and she didn't let it limit her. She was tired and had no appetite and sometimes it affected her mentally. If she became aware of depressive thoughts, she found new energy in starting to search for new music. But she hardly ever commented on her condition.

How did she react when she realized she was dying?
It is difficult to answer as I only spoke with her over the phone. But she spoke a lot about how much my friends and I meant to her.

Addendum

MERCEDES SOSA: *The Voice of Hope* is the first book ever written about Mercedes Sosa in English. I started out writing in my mother tongue, Danish, but as I came across people in the English-speaking community who loved Mercedes Sosa but hardly knew anything about her, I decided to switch to English, even though it was, of course, far more challenging.

In conducting my research, I got hold of all the information about Mercedes Sosa that I could in English. However, most of the material available to me was in Spanish. Not having access to Spanish sources seemed like a hindrance at first, but it soon turned out to be an advantage as it forced me to use all my senses. In order to make the story unique and personal, I decided to stick to my method of perceiving. I listened to Mercedes Sosa's songs and watched her on DVDs or on the Internet, and got to know her almost in the same way we get to know someone in real life. If we want to get to know someone, we spend time with them, listen to what they say, watch their expressions, and observe their behavior. We also do our best to understand what the other person is going through. This is how I got to know Mercedes Sosa. I have used a mindful approach in my research, which means I have spent hours in her company—nearly every day for six years, paying attention to her voice, expressions, gestures, and way of relating to others, while noticing the psychological and physical effect these observations had on myself. Furthermore, I have used the insight I gained about Mercedes to empathize with what it was like to be in her shoes. In the passage where I describe what ran through her head when the audience gave her a ten-minute standing ovation, I stood up, closed my eyes, listened to the cheers from a concert, and pretended I was Mercedes—until my husband asked me what on earth I was doing.

I used my imagination to strengthen the flow of the narrative or to highlight a point in the following passages:

Mercedes' reaction to Víctor Jara's death.

The fear response to the warning letter from Triple A.

Her thoughts on the journey back from exile.

Fearing what people will think of her being overweight, when watching herself in the mirror.

How she experienced the ten-minute standing ovation in Carnegie Hall.

The sleeplessness at the onset of her depression in 1997.

Mercedes' reflections about her life while studying her face in the window in 2007.

Waiting for Fabián to take her to the hospital.

The concerts I describe have elements from other concerts too.

Sometimes different sources stated different things on the same subject. It is therefore uncertain whether her drinking problem was right after her divorce or if it was during her exile.

It is unclear what caused the loss of her voice during exile. I researched the very rare phenomenon and found that it probably was a rise in gastric acid that caused the problem. Since this explanation is used when she lost her voice the second time during her depression, it is likely that it was the same cause that happened during exile. In medical terms, the diagnosis is called reflux laryngitis.

About the Author

ANETTE CHRISTENSEN, born and raised in Denmark, began her career by helping develop international charity programs. Later she became a language teacher for college students, and then, with her husband, ran a travel agency and a real estate agency. Now semi-retired and living in Turkey, she writes and focuses on personal growth.

For years Anette travelled in many parts of the world. Her experiences with various cultures have enabled her to engage with people with a different outlook on life than her own. She is eager to learn from others and finds joy in embracing the difference of others, spotting the uniqueness that she believes is within each individual.

The Mercedes Sosa

Foundation

In Argentina, Fabián Matus, Mercedes Sosa's son, and her two grandchildren, Agustín and Araceli, have been working hard and wholeheartedly to keep Mercedes Sosa's legacy alive. I am thrilled to have established a connection with this wonderful family and grateful for their support and appreciation of the book. Unfortunately, Fabían Matus died from cancer, only sixty years old, on March 15, 2019. Agustín and Araceli take on the torch.

The Mercedes Sosa Foundation is a non-profit cultural institution that seeks to preserve and spread the artistic heritage of Mercedes Sosa in order to promote and develop the Latin American culture in the current and new generations of Argentina and the rest of the world, through the many cultural activities that it offers. Visit mercedessosa.org

Endnotes

THANK YOU FOR the time you have spent getting to know both Mercedes Sosa and me. I hope you will move on from here with a strong sense of hope and of being welcome in this world. If this book has touched or inspired you in any way I'd be very grateful if you will share your reading experience with your network or leave a short review on Amazon or Goodreads. It will help others to receive the same benefits you have.

I'll also encourage you to visit my webpage mercedes-sosa.com or my facebook.com/AnetteChristensenAuthor for further inspiration. On my **You Tube Channel** named after the book, you'll find a selection of playlists with handpicked clips supporting the themes in the book. I hope you'll find them useful.

Songs and Episodes from the Book
Songs for Joy, Strength and Energy
Songs for Peace, Hope and Comfort
Performing with Other Artists
Full Concerts Chronological
The Beauty of Latin America
Latin American Politics and History
The Psychological Aspects
My Latin American Favorites

Recordings

Canciones con fundamento (1959)

La voz de la zafra (1961)

Hermano (1966)

Yo no canto por cantar (1966)

Para cantarle a mi gente (1967)

Con sabor a Mercedes Sosa (1968)

Mujeres argentinas (1969)

El grito de la tierra (1970)

Navidad con Mercedes Sosa (1970)

Güemes, el guerrillero del norte (1971)

Homenaje a Violeta Parra (1971)

Cantata Sudamericana (1972)

Hasta la victoria (1972)

Mercedes Sosa y Horacio Guarany (single 1973)

Traigo un pueblo en mi voz (1973)

Mercedes Sosa y Horacio Guarany (single 1974)

A que florezca mi pueblo (1975)

Niño de mañana (1975)

En dirección del viento (1976)

Mercedes Sosa (1976)

Mercedes Sosa interpreta a Atahualpa Yupanqui (1977)

O cio da terra (1977)

Serenata para la tierra de uno (1979)

Gravado ao vivo no Brasil (1980)

A quién doy (1981)

Mercedes Sosa en Argentina (1982)

Como un pájaro libre (1983)

Mercedes Sosa (1983)

Recital (1983)

¿Será posible el sur? (1984)

Corazón americano (1985) (con Milton Nascimento y León Gieco)

Vengo a ofrecer mi corazón (1985)

Mercedes Sosa '86 (1986)

Mercedes Sosa '87 (1987)

Gracias a la vida (1987)

Amigos míos (1988)

Live in Europa (1990)

De mí (1991)

30 años (1993)

Sino (1993)

Gestos de amor (1994)

Oro (1995)

Escondido en mi país (1996)

Alta fidelidad (1997) (con Charly García)

Al despertar (1998)

Misa Criolla (2000)

Acústico (2002)

Argentina quiere cantar (2003) (con Víctor Heredia y León Gieco)

Corazón libre (2005)

Cantora (2009)

Deja la vida volar (2010)

Censurada (2011)

Siempre en ti (2013)

Selva sola (2013)

Ángel (2014)

Lucerito (2015)

Sources

1. Mercedes Sosa has Died, October 4, 2009, Rachel Hall, *The Argentina Independent.*
2. Irgenwann singe ich John Lennon's Imagine, October 25, 2003, Hinnerk Berlekamp, berliner-zeitung.de.
3. *Cantora, un viaje intimo,* DVD.
4. *Mercedes Sosa, La voz de Latinoamérica,* DVD.
5. Tribute to Mercedes Sosa, October 2009, Renata Dikeopoulou,ghostradio.gr.
6. Tomamos la vida muy a la ligera, 1999, Víctor M. Amela, Solidaridad.net.
7. Mi canto latinoamericano, Claus Schreiner, 1988, Darmstadt.
8. *Mercedes Sosa La Negra,* Rodolfo Braceli, 2010, Penguin Random House.
9. *La Nueva Canción,* Smithsonian Folkways, The New Song Movement in South America.
10. Argentine Singing Legend Mercedes Sosa dies at 74, October 5, 2009, Adam Bernstein, *Washington Post.*
11. Mercedes Sosa, A Voice of Hope, October 9, 1988, Larry Rohter, *The New York Times.*
12. Argentina's Mercedes Sosa Emerges as a Survivor, October 22, 1988, Victor Valle, *Los Angeles Times.*
13. Mercedessosa.org.
14. The life and death of Víctor Jara, September 18, 2013, Andrew Tyler, *The Guardian.*
15. Argentine Singer Sosa's Power Outlasted Political Tyranny, January 14, 2011, Mike Quinn, Sounds Good.
16. Argentina Releases Nazi Files, February 4, 1992, articles.sun-sentinel.com.
17. *Searching for Life,* Rita Ardetti, 1999, University of California Press.

18. Secret Military Dictatorship's Documents Found in Basement, November 5, 2013, Tess Bennett, *The Argentina Independent.*

19. Mercedes Sosa Comes Back from the Pit, May 26, 1999, Utusan Online.

20. La Negra is back - with God at her side, June 6, 2007, Pablo Calvi, *Daily News.*

21. Folk Legend Mercedes Sosa Dies, October 9, 2009, *The Telegraph.*

22. Sosa's Land Always Near in her Songs, September 4, 2003, Sandra Hernandez, *Sunsentinel.*

23. *Como un Pájaro Libre*, by Ricardo Willicher, DVD.

24. *Singing Truth to Power: Mercedes Sosa, 1935–2009*, T.M. Scruggs, Nacla.

25. *Mercedes Sosa, Será possible el sur?* by Stefan Paul.

26. Grandmothers of Plaza de Mayo Find Child 126, December 6, 2017, *The Bubble, Argentina News*

27. Argentina's Diva of the Dispossessed, March 13, 2012, Tom Schnabel, blogs.kcrw.com.

28. Mercedes Sosa, song with no Boundaries, The Free Library.com.

29. Migrant Voice of Argentina, November 3, 1989, Geoffrey Himes, *Washington Post.*

30. *Earthcharter.org/discover.*

31. *Three Worlds, Three Voices, One Vision*, DVD.

32. Bruce Springsteen Helped Breach Berlin Wall, Rolling Stone Magazine, June 27, 2013, by Jon Blistein.

33. Live concert, in Boston, 1989, YouTube.

34. Show de Xuxa, Xuxa recipe Mercedes Sosa 1993, YouTube.

35. Mercedes Sosa: Cantora an Upright Last Offering, Tobias, Tokafi.com.

36. Qué puedo hacer si no es cantar?, 12, May 20, 2006, Karina Micheletto, pagina12.com.ar.

37. Mercedes Sosa, The Voice of the Voiceless Ones, December 12, 2011, Christel Veraart, Soundscapes, Blogspot.com.

38. Argentina's Diva of the Dispossessed, March 13, 2012, Tom Schnabel, blogs.kcrw.com.

39. Mercedes Sosa, Singer or Saint of the People, February 9, 2014, Sandra Bertrand, galomagazine.com.

40. Live concert, Jujuy - Argentina en vivo 1 and 2, March 2001, YouTube.

41. Mercedes Sosa, A Lifelong Source of Inspiration, October 9, 2009, Ian Malinow, *The Examiner*.

42. Argentine singer Mercedes Sosa Dies at 74, October 9, 2009, Helen Popper, Reuters.

43. Mercedes Sosa se emocionó con una serenata sorpresa, February 21. 2007, Clarin.com.

44. Serenata a la querida "Negra Sosa", ofrecida por el programa "Mp3, Música para el Tercer Milenio," conducido por el "Bahiano," parte 1 and 2.

45. Famed Argentine Folk Singer Mercedes Sosa Hospitalized, breathing with a respirator, October 1, 2009, entertainment.gaeatimes.com.

46. Argentine Singer, Mercedes Sosa, in Grave Condition, October 3, 2009, Latin American Herald Tribune, laht.com.

47. Mercedes Sosa, Who Sang of Argentina's turmoil Dies, October 5, 2009, Larry Rohter, The New York Times.

48. How Stress Affects your Brain, Madhumita Murgia, TED.com.

49. Cortisol in Control? Oxytocin to the Rescue for a More Loving, Healthier Life, Drannacabeca.com.

50. The Neurobiology of We, Patty de Llosa, 2011.

51. Using The Social Engagement System, Nov. 13.2012, Tom Bunn, *Psychology Today*.

52. This is your Brain on Music, April 15, 2013, Elizabeth Landau, CNN.

53. Mercedes Sosa Captivates with substance and Style, November, 13, 2005, David Cazares, *Sun Sentinel*

Bibliography

Books

The Penguin History of Latin America, Edwin Williamson, 1992, Penguin Group

Searching for Life, Rita Ardetti, 1999, University of California Press

Mi canto latinoamericano, Claus Schreiner, 1988, Darmstadt

Mercedes Sosa La Negra, Rodolfo Braceli, 2010, Penguin Random House

From Distress to De-stress, Pauline Skeates and Sandy Fabrin, 2010, Insight services Ltd

Wherever You Go There You Are, Jon Kabat-Zinn, 2004, Hyperion

The Compassionate Mind, Paul Gilbert, 2010, Constable & Robinson Ltd

DVDs

Mercedes Sosa, Será possible el sur? by Stefan Paul

Como un Pájaro Libre by Ricardo Willicher

Three Worlds, Three Voices, One Vision

Mercedes Sosa, Acústico en Suiza

Cantora, un viaje intimo

Mercedes Sosa, La voz de Latinoamérica

Web Sites

Mercedes Sosa: Cantora an Upright Last Offering, Tobias, Tokafi.com

Folk Legend Mercedes Sosa Dies, October 9, 2009, The Telegraph

Mercedes Sosa, Who Sang of Argentina's turmoil, Dies, October 5, 2009, Larry Rohter, The New York Times

Mercedes Sosa, A Voice of Hope, October 9, 1988, Larry Rother, The New York Times

Argentine Singing Legend Mercedes Sosa dies at 74, October 5, 2009, Adam Bernstein, Washington Post

Argentina's Mercedes Sosa Emerges as a Survivor, October 22, 1988, Victor Valle, Los Angeles Times

Argentina's Rebel-Rousing Diva, May 16, 2001, Robin Denselow, The Guardian

Mercedes Sosa obituary, October 5, Garth Cartwright, The Guardian

Argentine singer Mercedes Sosa Dies at 74, October 9, 2009, Helen Popper, Reuters

Mercedes Sosa has Died, October 4, 2009, Rachel Hall, The Argentina Independent

Cumplo mi promesa, Martin Peres, Pagina 12.com

Secret Military Dictatorship's Documents Found in Basement, November 5, 2013, Tess Bennett, The Argentina Independent

La Nueva Canción, Smithsonian Folkways, The New Song Movement in South America

Irgenwann singe ich John Lennon's Imagine, October 25, 2003, Hinnerk Berlekamp, berliner-zeitunq.de

Tribute to Mercedes Sosa, October 2009, Renata Dikeopoulou, ghostradio.gr

Famed Argentine Folk Singer Mercedes Sosa Hospitalized, breathing with a respirator, October 1, 2009, entertainment.gaeatimes.com

Argentine Singer, Mercedes Sosa, in Grave Condition, October 3, 2009, Latin American Herald Tribune, laht.com

Mercedes Sosa Remains Grave with "Deterioration of Organ Functions," Latin American Herald Tribune, laht.com

Sosa's Land Always Near in her Songs, September 4, 2003, Sandra Hernandez, Sun Sentinel

Argentina's Diva of the Dispossessed, March 13, 2012, Tom Schnabel, blogs.kcrw.com

Mercedes Sosa, Singer or Saint of the People, February 9, 2014, Sandra Bertrand, galomagazine.com

Cantora, Mercedes Sosa, Fernando Gonzalez, irom.wordpress.com

Qué puedo hacer si no es cantar?, 12, May 20, 2006, Karina Micheletto, pagina12.com.ar

The neurobiology of We, Patty de Llosa, 2011

Mercedes Sosa, a compelling figure in world music and a social activist, October 29, 1995, Don Heckman, Los Angeles Times

Political Controversy Won't Keep Sosa Out of Miami, November 3, 1989, John Lennart, Sun Sentinel

Argentina Releases Nazi Files, February 4, 1992, articles.sun-sentinel.com

Migrant Voice of Argentina, November 3, 1989, Geoffrey Himes, Washington Post

Mission Justice - Argentina, Human Rights Violations in Argentina, August 9, 2010, Drew Gillespie, missionjusticeargentina.blogspot.com.tr

This is your brain on music, April 15, 2013, Elizabeth Landau, CNN

The Science of Love, Barbara Fredrickson, Aeon Magazine

Blending politics and music, October 21, 2009, Bridget Broderick, Socialistworker.org

Mercedes Sosa, The Voice of the Voiceless Ones, December 12, 2011, Christel Veraart, Soundscapes, Blogspot.com

Argentina Plaza de Mayo Grandmothers find child 119, December 1, 2015, BBC News

Film: Será Posible el Sur?, On an Argentine Singer, September 11, 1987, Jon Pareles, The New York Times

Earthcharter.org/discover

The life and death of Víctor Jara, September 18, 2013, Andrew Tyler, The Guardian

Argentine Singer Sosa's Power Outlasted Political Tyranny, January 14, 2011, Mike Quinn, Sounds Good

Singing Truth to Power: Mercedes Sosa, 1935–2009, T.M. Scruggs, Nacla

Bruce Springsteen Helped Breach Berlin Wall, June 27, 2013, Jon Blitstein

Mercedes Sosa, Songs with no Boundaries, June 1996, Caleb Bach, Questia.com

Mercedes Sosa Captivates with substance and Style, November, 13, 2005, David Cazares, Sun Sentinel

Tomamos la vida muy a la ligera, 1999, Victor M. Amela, Solidaridad.net

Mercedes Sosa se emocionó con una serenata sorpresa, February 21. 2007, Clarin.com

La Negra is back – with God at her side, June 6, 2007, Pablo Calvi, Daily News

Mercedes Sosa Comes Back From the Pit, May 26, 1999, Utusan Online

Argentina's Mercedes Sosa – She died in Peace, a Free Woman, Georgianne Nienaber, Huffington Post

Using The Social Engagement System, Nov. 13, 2012, Tom Bunn, Psychology Today

How Stress Affects your Brain, Madhumita Murgia, TED.com

Mercedes Sosa, A Lifelong Source of Inspiration, October 9, 2009, Ian Malinow, The Examiner

Cortisol in Control? Oxytocin to the Rescue for a More Loving, Healthier Life, Drannacabeca.com

The Science and Art of Presence: How Being Open and Receptive to Life Cultivates Well-Being, Daniel Siegel, Mindsightinstitute.com

Santiago Maldonado, Missing backpacker takes center stage in Argentina's elections, Oct. 6, 2017, Uki Goñi, The Guardian

Argentina. A 23 años del asesinato del periodista Mario Bonino, el crimen continúa impune, Resumen, Nov. 12, 2016

Interviews

Christel Verarrt, composer-singer, Alaska

Fernando Pellegrini, journalist, Argentina

Luis Plaza Ibarra, Musician, Gothenburg, Sweden

Ignacio Zamalloa Markovic, Actor, La Plata, Buenos Aires

Photo Credits

Manufactured by Amazon.ca
Bolton, ON

24690505R00127